Motivational Quotes

By Vince Baker
& Smith Wigglesworth

> **Show me someone who did something great in this life and I will show you a person who lived by or came up with many powerful quotes!**

Scripture quotations are taken from the Holy Bible, King James Version. The King James Version is public domain in the United States of America. All bolding and emphasis are added by the author.

Printed in the United States of America

Table of Content

Smith Wigglesworth Quotes

Introduction

The quotes in this book have changed my life, and I believe they will change the life of anyone who not only reads but receives the wisdom found in each quote. God is having me share this book now to encourage and strengthen the body of Christ with these motivational and inspirational quotes.

It all started when I was seventeen, driving in my car. God manifested Himself to me in such a powerful way it was undeniable. After this experience I asked my mom to lead me to the Lord, and she at that time was also having a revival of her own. Within a few days, it was my birthday, and my grandmother gave me a book about Smith Wigglesworth called *The Secret of His Power.* This book impacted me and set the course of my Christian life.

God started talking to me more about what He wanted to do in my life from many of the things I read about in Smith Wigglesworth's life. The catch was that it wouldn't happen until later in my life. In the meantime, God told me to prepare myself, which is exactly what I did. I ended up going to Bible college and graduating Valedictorian. I memorized hundreds of Bible verses. I also worked with an Evangelist and became his right-hand man as we traveled up and down the West Coast, teaching the Church how to Evangelize the homeless with the power of God.

A part of my preparation came in the form of quotes. I wrote down and studied quotes from Smith Wigglesworth that highly impacted my life. One of his famous quotes is, "I am not moved by what I see or hear but by what I believe." If you know anything about Smith Wigglesworth, you will find he came up with many powerful quotes. He would say these one-liners that could infuse faith in people. What made them so impactful was the life he lived, and the miracles God did through him.

I also wrote down and studied every quote I could find from anyone throughout history who was famous or did something to impact this world. It took me a long time, but I noticed how my faith grew, and I became stronger as I meditated on these powerful quotes. We are made up mostly of what we think, and if you keep filling your mind with the Word of God and powerful quotes, you will see wonderful changes in your life.

As time passed, one day, God said to me, "Why don't you come up with your own quotes." This was such a novel idea that I had never thought about. What happened next was utterly amazing! God started downloading me with quotes, and I couldn't write them down fast enough. Whenever the quote would come to me, I would make sure not to lose it. This went on for years, and it still happens to me. I believe I have somewhere around 1,500 quotes now, and all of them came from God.

The closest person I can relate to in this is King Solomon. When God gave King Solomon wisdom, he wrote down over 3,000 Proverbs. A quote is close to a proverb. God gave me quotes like He gave King

Solomon proverbs. I cannot take any credit for the quotes in this book. I give God ALL the glory. Whenever I go back over the quotes God gave me, they continue to profoundly affect me.

God revealed to me that a quote based on His Word can pack a lot of power in a time of need. A perfectly timed quote can defeat demonic thoughts from the enemy. Quotes become useful when you are at a crossroads in your life and need encouragement and direction. A quote is like a whole sermon in and of itself.

You will notice as you study great men of God or influential leaders of the past, they each had their own quotes that motivated them. Every great man or woman of God was filled with powerful quotes they either received from someone else or invented on their own. History is packed with amazing people who lived and died by the quotes they believed in.

Every person who became a historical legend had a stack of quotes they used to bring them to greatness. Show me a person who studies and creates inspiring motivational quotes, and I will show you someone who does extraordinary things. Motivational quotes can alter history by how they impact those who hear and receive them. Ordinary people can become extraordinary by changing how they think through the power of Divine quotes. Sometimes, all it takes is a perfectly timed quote to alter someone's destiny.

Once you start becoming the quotes you are reading or coming up with on your own, you are never the same. There will be a remarkable difference in how you think, speak, and act if you allow

God to use wise quotes that are Biblically based to change you from the inside out. Never underestimate how Divine quotes can impact you in ways that go beyond the normal course of life.

I pray this book encourages and blesses you to where you do incredible things for God and fulfill your High Calling. May the God of Heaven BLESS You through our Lord and Saviour Jesus Christ and by the power of the Holy Spirit.

66 *It's amazing how a small one-liner quote can change the world.*

Vince Baker

Vince Baker

Quotes

CHAPTER 1

Anointing

❝The anointing will not cost you any money, but it will cost you everything else.

The anointing will make you a superhero.

The true anointing is not a gimmick but only works by truly knowing God.

The Anointing is in the Word.

Unfaithfulness will steal the Anointing of God on your life.

Always remember that the anointing is there to meet other people's needs.

You cannot stay anointed if you don't stay obedient.

Walking in a powerful and stabilized anointing on this earth takes years of preparation.

When the anointing comes on someone, they will have abilities they never had before.

Every anointing comes with a charge from the Lord.

The anointing is placed upon someone so they can keep the charge of the Lord.

To walk in God's Anointing, you must be bold, strong, and confident.

A measure of faith and the Holy Spirit working through someone is the anointing.

You can receive blessings from God when you believe in the Anointing from God on someone else.

Anointed men and women are the move of God.

If you are faithful during times of testing, God will unleash a powerful anointing through you.

When someone walking in the anointing walks into a situation, the foundation of all reality is shifted to what God has destined to happen through faith.

To walk in a strong anointing, you must be willing to open the floodgates of giving.

The anointing is all about giving to others and protecting others.

The greater the faith you have, the greater the anointing you will have.

You cannot tame an anointed man of God on a mission.

The world's problems are no match for a faith-filled anointed man of God.

It takes an anointed way of thinking to operate in the anointing.

Anointed people think like the Holy Spirit.

The anointing will make you a legend.

Anointed sons of God have the power to manifest who they are to be transformed into right now.

When God anoints you, He weaponizes your words.

66 **When someone is operating in a high anointing, others may feel insignificant because of the High Honor God is placing upon the one anointed.**

Ministers who operate in a powerful anointing must make sure they give all of the glory to God because of the temptation to fall into pride because of how people will look up to them.

Always follow the Anointing of the Spirit of God, and don't make the Anointing of the Spirit follow you.

You must let God create the full image of Christ within you before you can walk in the fullness of the anointing on your life.

Times of testing are necessary to see if you are fully matured into the image of Christ and if you can handle the anointing and all of the temptations that come with it.

When the miracles, signs, and wonders start flowing through you naturally, people will know you are an anointed son of God.

The amount of Anointing that God can flow through your life is in proportion to the image of God that has been transformed within you.

You cannot operate in the full capacity of the anointing until you are fully walking in the image of a mature son of God.

Anyone walking in a heavy anointing from God will be filled with the deep wisdom of God.

One of the fastest ways to lose the anointing is to start acting like a fool.

One of the fastest ways to be anointed by God is to walk in God's wisdom.

The anointing works best under pressure.

The anointing works best when there are great needs.

The anointing works best when helping people going through fiery trials and needing help.

I have never seen anyone walk in a heavy anointing that has a spirit of levity.

The anointing has an answer to every problem.

An anointed man or woman of God will find an answer from the Holy Spirit for all the problems the devil throws at them.

The anointing gives you an unfair advantage over the enemy.

If you want to be anointed by God, you need to make vows to God and keep them.

" *The anointing of God is given to defeat enemies.*

Many moving parts in the Spirit have to be understood, built, and functioning before you can operate in a powerful anointing.

1 John 2:27 (KJV)
But the anointing which ye have received of him abideth in you, and ye need not that any man teach you: but as the same anointing teacheth you of all things, and is truth, and is no lie, and even as it hath taught you, ye shall abide in him.

CHAPTER 2

Charge of the Lord

❝Every anointing comes with a very specific Charge from the Lord.

Before God blesses you to enter your Promised Land, He will give you a Charge. Make sure you keep and obey it.

Many responsibilities, blessings, and consequences come with the Charge of the Lord.

The Bible is filled with examples of how people were blessed or cursed, even unto death, depending on whether they kept the Charge of the Lord or not.

God wants to see who will pick up His call, mandate, and Charge.

God is looking to see who can be trusted and who will be faithful to their call, mandate, and Charge.

Everything in God's Kingdom is given a Charge from the Lord.

If you keep the Charge of the Lord, God will be with you.

Deuteronomy 11:1 (KJV)
Therefore thou shalt love the Lord thy God, and keep his charge, and his statutes, and his judgments, and his commandments, alway.

CHAPTER 3

Church

❝Since the resurrection of Jesus Christ, the Church is mandated to take back the nations from the devil.

When it gets bad enough, the world will be looking for God and a powerful Church to pray over them and raise their family members from the dead.

The Church was born to be a victorious army.

The biggest enemy of the Church is sometimes the Church.

There is just as much evil in the Church as there is on the outside of the Church right now.

Make sure you rebuke and cast out any witch or warlock trying to operate in the Church and feel good about it.

For the Church to be victorious, it has to get away from a defensive mindset and move to an offensive mindset.

Every Church lives in the Gospel that they preach.

1 Timothy 3:15 (KJV)
But if I tarry long, that thou mayest know how thou oughtest to behave thyself in the house of God, which is the church of the living God, the pillar and ground of the truth.

CHAPTER 4

Commitment

"Everything you are looking for is hidden behind a total sold-out commitment to God and His Kingdom.

Everything you seek is hidden behind a deep, unfailing commitment to Christ.

God speaks and reveals greater revelations to those who commit their whole spirit, soul, body, affections, and strength to Him.

The more profound revelations of God are hidden behind deeper commitments to God.

Commitment to Christ has to be walked out every second, minute, and hour of the day.

Proverbs 16:3 (KJV)
Commit thy works unto the Lord, and thy thoughts shall be established.

CHAPTER 5

Complaining

❝Murmuring and complaining are the first stages of betrayal.

Complaining is the beginning stage of quitting.

Complaining is a form of quitting.

Complainers usually end up being quitters.

Complainers become quitters, quitters become backsliders, and backsliders become reprobate enemies of God.

Thankful people make no room for complaining.

Thankfulness is the polar opposite of complaining.

Philippians 2:14 (KJV)
Do all things without murmurings and disputings:

CHAPTER 6

✦

Conscience

❝You don't need anyone else to beat you up when you sin because your conscience can do a very good job at that.

Your conscience can be your best friend or your worst enemy.

Your conscience is not always right, but it's never right to go against your conscience.

Never do anything that would harm the integrity of your conscience.

True repentance, wisdom, and the Blood of Jesus Christ are the only ways to cleanse a guilty conscience.

Your conscience helps you to stay faithful to God.

Maintaining a clean conscience keeps you from being a hypocrite.

If you fall, quickly repent, get back up, and ask God to cleanse your conscience by the Blood of Jesus.

When your conscience confirms that the Spirit is truly leading you, you are in a great place of confidence and strength.

A clean conscience is the strongest foundation if one wants God to hear and answer their prayers.

Hebrews 9:14 (KJV)
How much more shall the blood of Christ, who through the eternal Spirit offered himself without spot to God, purge your conscience from dead works to serve the living God?

CHAPTER 7

Courage & Boldness

❝Never fear the enemy's retaliation when you walk in the boldness of God.

Some of the greatest commodities during a crisis are faith, courage, and boldness.

Boldness is a weapon in and of itself.

Boldness is a form of protection in and of itself.

Speaking boldly is a big part of spiritual warfare.

Prophetic insight into the future creates great boldness.

You must attack fear and eradicate it at every level within yourself until nothing but pure boldness remains.

If you listen to fear, you will be dominated by the devil.

You can get to a place in your boldness in God that you don't feel any fear.

To be more than a conqueror, you must have strong courage.

Courage is a choice.

Boldness is a shield of protection.

Courage in the Lord is the weapon that can help you defeat your enemies.

Don't fear being strong because it will always work in your favor when you are in right standing with God.

Being strong and courageous in the Lord always works out in your favor.

Unless you are raptured out of here, die bold.

You must be bold and strong about everything the Lord has taught you.

There are great blessings to be found in being bold.

If you spend time with Jesus, you will get bold.

Eradicate all fear until only pure boldness remains.

Acts 4:13 (KJV)
Now when they saw the boldness of Peter and John, and perceived that they were unlearned and ignorant men, they marvelled; and they took knowledge of them, that they had been with Jesus.

CHAPTER 8

*

Covenant

❝When you are in Covenant with God, you can be afraid of something that you do not need to be afraid of because God will defend you.

You cannot get close to the Lord if you won't get into and keep a Covenant with Him.

Your Covenant with God is your most valuable possession.

The Covenant of God is voice-activated by faith.

Just because you don't inherit the promise of God doesn't mean the Covenant of God didn't pay for it.

Jesus walked in an unusual level of confidence and faith because He understood the Covenant of God.

It's hard to find good revelatory teaching and preaching on the Everlasting New Covenant of God.

Anyone who fully understands the New Covenant will walk in an unusual confidence, faith, and anointing.

Making and keeping a Covenant with God is the most wonderful thing you can do.

We enter into the blood Covenant of Jesus by cutting a Covenant with our mouth by confessing Jesus as our Lord.

Jesus died on the cross not because God broke the Covenant but because man broke the Covenant.

Covenants are a big deal, and God Himself would be punished if He broke His own Covenant with mankind.

There is nothing more special than being in Covenant with God.

The most wonderful thing you can do is stand in Covenant with God and never back down.

The Covenant of God is the most beautiful thing in the world.

The best thing you can do in this life is get in a deep Covenant with God through Jesus Christ.

Your Covenant with God is worth giving your life and dying for.

A big part of the Covenant of God is He will forgive your sins.

When a believer sins, they break Covenant with God.

All sin is making a Covenant with the devil.

The blood of Jesus was the cost for God to make a Covenant with those who believe.

Faith is the only way to access the Covenant God made with Jesus.

You have to put on Christ by faith and not fulfill the lust of the flesh to access the Covenant of God.

In the New Covenant, the Holy Spirit writes the Laws of God on your heart.

The Lord will keep Covenant with you as you keep Covenant with Him.

You have to keep yourself in the Covenant of God if you want to partake of the promises of God.

Your conscience plays a big role in the New Covenant.

"*If you violate your conscience, you violate the New Covenant.***

God expects you to be perfect, harmless, unblameable, unrebukable, undefiled, and without spot in the New Covenant.

God will do anything and everything to keep and fulfill the Covenant that He has made.

God honors those who honor His Covenants.

God can only trust you if you are in Covenant with Him.

The wisest thing you can do in this life is get in and keep a Covenant with God.

All Biblical teachings are incomplete without the Covenant of God understanding intermixed at their foundation.

Your Covenant with God is wrapped up with your Covenant with your spouse.

If you break Covenant with your spouse, you break Covenant with God.

If you cannot verbally confess your vows to God, you are not in Covenant with God.

True Covenant love has the ability to make and keep vows to God.

Make a vocally loud Covenant with God, and God will be there for you in your time of need.

You can't tempt a faithful man who has made a soul-binding Covenant with His God.

God deals with everyone according to His Covenant.

Never break your Eternal Covenant with God for anything or anyone.

Never let a woman get in between you and your Covenant with God Almighty.

You can break Covenant with God by lusting after the beauty of a woman.

All lust will cause you to violate your Covenant with God.

You have to protect and guard your Covenant with God with your life.

You cannot be fully trusted if you are unwilling to make a verbal Covenant with God.

The power of God backs the Covenant of God.

You are either in Covenant with, have no Covenant with God, or are breaking the Covenant of God.

You can access the Covenant of God through someone anointed by faith.

It is a privilege to be in Covenant with God.

Your Eternal Everlasting Covenant with God starts in this life.

The Everlasting Covenant with God starts with your confession as Jesus being your Lord.

The Holy Spirit was sent to help you see, get in, and keep the Covenant God made with Jesus.

Jesus originally started healing people based on the Covenant that God made with Abraham to bless the world.

The Covenant of God protects you from everything.

The devil works hard to keep people from seeing the Covenant of God.

66 *Covenants with God are made with your mouth.*

The devil works hard to try to get people not to understand the Covenant of God.

The devil works hard to try to get people to break their Covenant with God.

All devils are covenant-breakers.

You cannot access the promises of God if you are not in Covenant with God.

The promises of God can only be accessed by those who are in Covenant with Him.

Agape love and Covenant are one and the same in the Bible.

To understand the Covenant of God, you must understand the Agape love of God.

Jesus did not die on the cross to make a Covenant with angels but with fallen humanity.

The New Covenant was only made between God and humans.

God is very serious about His Covenants.

The New Covenant with Christ can only be accessed by faith.

The Spirit of grace reveals God's Covenant to you and enables you to keep it.

You have to make your own Covenant with the Covenant God made with Jesus to be saved and used by God.

You will come up with crazy teachings and doctrines if you don't understand the New Covenant.

❝If you disobey any of the teachings of Christ, you violate the New Covenant.

God expresses and reveals His love in the Covenants He makes.

Everything you read about in the Bible has to do with God's Covenants.

The gifts of the Spirit are the fulfillment of the promises of God in the New Covenant.

God is not obligated to help you if you are not in Covenant with Him.

God made a Covenant with Himself through Abraham to Jesus Christ.

God's Covenants encapsulate all that He is.

You have to die to yourself to get into Covenant with God.

You have to die daily to stay in Covenant with God.

The New Covenant is a verbal soul-binding promise to God that you confess that Jesus is your Lord by faith, agreeing to obey all He says and vowing to stop sinning by keeping a pure conscience free from the lusts of the flesh before God.

Everything you say and do should be based on your Covenant with God.

The Dunamis power of God only backs the Covenant of God.

The Holy Spirit was sent to help the Church keep the New Covenant.

Staying daily in the word and prayer keeps you in remembrance of the New Covenant.

The temple was established as a portal of the Covenant between God and man.

The deeper the Covenant you make with God, the more powerful He can use you.

The nature of God is revealed in the Covenants He makes.

Repentance and faith are the only ways to access the New Covenant.

It is disgusting to see the things people choose over the Covenant of God.

Just saying and calling upon the name of the Lord Jesus Christ of Nazareth can activate the New Covenant.

All the teachings of Jesus are found in the Ark of the New Covenant.

Every man that God used was a Covenant man.

❝You cannot operate in the anointing if you don't understand the New Covenant.

Water baptism is a public sign of entering into the New Covenant.

Water baptism is a sign that you are dying to sin and coming alive to God in the New Covenant.

The baptism of Jesus by John the Baptist activated the Covenant that God made with Abraham.

Water baptism is symbolic of people dying to sin and coming up as a new person in the New Covenant that God made with Jesus when He raised Him from the dead.

The preaching of the cross is the preaching of the New Covenant.

Satan tempted Jesus to break Covenant with God when He was in the wilderness.

Jesus never broke His Covenant with God the Father.

Everything you read in the Bible has to do with God's Covenants.

The Cross of Christ did away with the Old Covenant when He died and ushered in the New Covenant when He rose from the dead.

The New Covenant is not one-sided; there are things you are also responsible for.

As you hold God to His Covenant, He will hold you to your Covenant to Him.

The Lord is in Covenant with you while you are in Covenant with Him.

Once you fully understand and walk in the New Covenant, you can activate it with your words.

Romans 11:27 (KJV)
For this is my Covenant unto them, when I shall take away their sins.

CHAPTER 9

Cross

❝ What you do with the Cross of Christ will define your whole life.

The preaching of the message of the Cross releases the power of God.

The mystery of the Cross is the secret mystery of the Christian Life.

Every time you take up your Cross and die to yourself, you obtain more authority from God.

The event of the Cross of Christ establishes what it means to be a Christian.

You must take up your Cross and die daily to hear God speak to you at a higher level.

There are many mysteries of the Cross yet to be discovered.

The devil is afraid of people coming to a full understanding of what Jesus did on the Cross for them.

Declaring what God has done through the death, burial, and resurrection of Jesus Christ releases the power of God's Spirit.

When you fully understand all that occurred on the Cross, you will walk in the power of God.

The message of the Cross is the power of God.

The power of the Spirit of God is released through the preaching of the Cross.

The preaching of the Cross is the releasing of God's power.

The preaching of the Gospel restores humankind from the curse.

God expects us to put all of our faith in what was accomplished by the death, burial, and resurrection of Jesus.

Galatians 6:14 (KJV)
But God forbid that I should glory, save in the cross of our Lord Jesus Christ, by whom the world is crucified unto me, and I unto the world.

CHAPTER 10

❖

Destiny

❝You need to pray for wisdom so you don't do something stupid in this life that affects your eternal destiny.

The irony of your walk with God is that when you finally get to the point where you feel you are unworthy and helpless, you are starting to get closer to your destiny and ready to have a real impact on the world.

It's a dangerous thing to quit on your destiny.

Jeremiah 29:11 (KJV)
11 For I know the thoughts that I think toward you, saith the Lord, thoughts of peace, and not of evil, to give you an expected end.

CHAPTER 11

⬥

Enemy

❝ The only place the devil belongs in your life is either behind you or under your feet.

If the enemy can supernaturally wipe you out, God can supernaturally bless you.

Every Christian needs a worthy enemy or opponent to defeat.

I never want the devil to say that I made Vince Baker quit.

When the Lord is with you, you don't need to fear ANYTHING the devil throws at you.

The devil will make you want to run out of a place when you are just about to be delivered.

The Anointing scares the hell out of demons.

It's easy to get a devil but hard to get rid of them.

Never play mister nice guy with a devil.

Never get in unity with a devil.

Never feel sorry for a devil.

You can't reason with a demon.

Don't waste your time talking to a demon.

Never lay hands on a devil.

Don't let demons get comfortable being near you.

Don't eat with or entertain devils.

Don't make excuses for a devil.

The only thing devils are good for is to be cast out.

Never speak softly to a demon.

Never let a devil deceive you into disobeying God.

Never let a devil steal from you.

Never let a devil kill you.

Never let a devil destroy your life.

Never look at things that the devil wants you to look at.

Never study things the devil wants you to study.

Never let a demon mesmerize you.

Never hang out where the devil likes to hang out.

❝*Never speak what the devil is saying.*❞

Never make a pack with a demon.

Never submit to a devil.

Never play with a devil.

Never play games with a devil.

Never listen to the wisdom of a devil.

Cast out and down everything evil, wicked, lustful, fearful, and unbelieving thought the devil throws at you.

Never underestimate demons and their ability to deceive you.

Never go into battle with a demon without the Armor of God.

Never get prideful after you cast out and defeat a demon.

Never get under a demon.

Never work for a demonized jezebelic spirit.

Never back off when you have a demon on the run.

Never take pity on a demon.

Never forget that the devil uses people to do his will.

Never let a demon use you.

Never let a demon in your temple.

Never tell a devil your secrets.

Never fear what a devil speaks to you unless you are not living right with God.

Never let a devil prophesy over you.

Never let a demonized doctor tell you when you are going to die.

Never let a demonized doctor speak curses into your life and health.

Never let a demonized person lay hands on you.

Never let a devil speak into or over your life.

Never let a devil tell you your future.

Never believe what a demon says about your future.

Never let the devil use you to hurt someone.

Never sympathize with a demon.

Never make an allegiance with a devil.

Never let a demon curse you.

Never joke around with a demonized person.

Never let a demon speak through you.

Never believe or tolerate the curses hurled at you by a demonized person.

Never look at or meditate on demonized people.

❝Never meditate on what the devil says about ANYTHING.

Never meditate on what the devil says about ANYONE.

Never believe or listen to the gossip of devils.

Never fear a devil if you are in right standing with God.

Never let a devil entertain you.

Never entertain devils.

Never let a devil teach you.

Never let the devil break your hedge.

Never let a demon use up your time.

Never let a devil distract you.

Never let a devil steal your strength.

Never let a witch or warlock speak into or over your life.

Never let a devil talk you out of keeping all of your standards.

Never let a devil cause you not to trust your gut instinct.

Never let a devil get you to disobey and go against your conscience.

Never let the devil entrap you.

Never let a demon lead you astray.

Never believe a devil that tells you that you have no power or authority over him.

Never believe a devil that tells you that you cannot repent and get right with God.

Never believe a devil that tells you there is no hope for you.

Never pray for a devil because there is no hope for them.

Never be deceived by a demon speaking through a Christian.

Stay away from snakes, especially ones that speak.

Never let a snake bite you.

Never let a demonized person watch your kids, even if they are a family member.

Never let a demon around your kids.

Talking to devils is just a waste of time.

Quit acting like an immature little devil.

Demons and devils only respond to true authority and power.

Demons only obey someone who has real spiritual authority and power from God.

Make sure all demons are out of you before you try to get a demon out of someone else.

❝You are kidding yourself if you don't think demons are studying you to find out how to get past your armor and weaken you.

Your goal in God is to get where the devil fears you.

You can't get any truth out of a devil.

Quit acting like a devil.

Make sure your voice is not used as a portal of satan.

Disobedience to God will make you a habitation of devils.

Disobedient spirits can enter into disobedient people.

Fallen angels are jealous of the true sons of God.

The devil is not compatible with the Word of God.

The Word of God will shake the devil out of you.

Holy Ghost laughter scares the hell out of the devil.

There is no need to ask a devil a bunch of questions because they are all liars.

The devil will try to fill your head with thoughts that he wants you to speak so he can defeat you.

The devil will make you feel like there is a problem when there is no problem.

The devil likes to set "Honey Traps" on the people of God to get them to sin and then leverage their sin against them and always keep them down and weak.

You better find and repent of your weaknesses before the devil uses them against you.

A big part of the devil's game plan is to attack your mind with worry about things that may never happen.

One of the greatest times to prove your love for God is when the devil comes to test you while you are in the desert.

You have a great opportunity to put the devil in his place when he comes to challenge your obedience to God.

Roman armor will never protect you from a devil.

The devil is no match for a man or woman of God dressed in the Armor of God on the battlefield.

The devil comes in to steal your relationship with God through disobedience and defilement because he knows it will cause you to lose your authority and position with God.

Sometimes, family members are used more of the devil in people's lives than outside enemies.

A little wedge in your hedge is all the devil needs to start to destroy your life.

Distractions are some of the biggest enemies of a Christian.

When God is with you, He makes your enemies fight and defeat each other.

Sometimes, the Lord uses your enemies to get you where you need to be.

❝ *Make sure you are wearing God's armor when you go to war because it's supernatural, and trust me, you don't want to face the devil in human armor or naked.*

Some beautiful women are used as portals of satan to draw men away to their deaths.

Never allow yourself to be seduced by demonic beauty.

If you want devils in your life, have sex outside of marriage.

If you don't want demons in your life, keep your body sexually pure.

Never have sex with a witch unless you love devils.

Never give your strength to a demonized woman.

The devil likes to throw symptoms on people and see if they will talk about them so they will be stuck with the sickness.

The devil likes to oppress a person with a fearful thought that seems real to see if they will believe it and speak it and make it their reality.

Never let the devil bear down upon you a reality that does not align with God's Word, will, and promises.

God is the only person who can get a demon out of your life through the power of the Holy Spirit.

Always make the devil repay and restore sevenfold whatever he steals from you.

Never let a devil pray for you.

Never listen to, read, or watch demonic news.

It takes a stronger man or woman of God to cast out a strong demon.

Never fear the wrath of the devil because God's wrath is greater.

What the devil puts in your path to hinder you, God uses as stepping stones into the blessing and call of God on your life.

Never fear the anger or rage of a devil when you are right with God.

Nothing gives me more pleasure than putting a devil in his place.

God wants you to hear the thoughts of fear the enemy has because your enemy knows God is with you and what He is about to do to them.

There is no greater feeling than to be able to confidently laugh in the Holy Spirit while facing danger and your enemy.

Romans 16:20 (KJV)
And the God of peace shall bruise Satan under your feet shortly. The grace of our Lord Jesus Christ be with you. Amen.

CHAPTER 12

※

Faith

❝I don't want you to tell me how much faith you have; I want you to show the devil how much faith you have by defeating him in every battle.

The faith of Jesus alone could get the job done, but He still required others to have faith.

God doesn't determine when a miracle will occur; faith does.

Faith doesn't take no for an answer when it comes to the promises of God.

Even if God anointed you with a double portion of His Spirit, if you don't have faith, it won't do you a bit of good.

Jesus never lost a faith fight.

Faith legally grants God the ability to work a miracle on your behalf.

It's not until the essence of your life is in danger that you find out if you have faith or not.

Faith doesn't see delays or having to wait on God for an answer to prayer as a problem.

The main difference between someone weak in faith and someone strong in faith is what they think in their heart and what comes out of their mouth.

Faith always delivers a glorious ending to every test.

Faith violently takes by force what is promised to it in the Word of God.

Faith loves to get right in the middle of the worst possible situations and believe God for a miracle.

Faith knows that God will always come through, even if it gets down to the wire.

Unbelief is thinking, feeling, speaking, and believing you don't have something that God said you have.

Faith is not afraid of anything!

If it wasn't for Jesus, we wouldn't have any faith.

Make sure God marvels at your faith and not your unbelief.

There is no such thing as faith that doesn't love to be challenged.

The wind does all the work for an eagle in a storm, and so does God for those who wait upon Him in faith and prayer.

Great faith brings great answers.

Faith will produce miracles, but miracles will never produce faith; only the Word of God produces faith in us.

If you're not going to believe God to the end, then you didn't have faith.

Faith will fight the devil and say, no, not today satan.

Faith is the only thing that says no to the devil stealing, killing, and trying to destroy your life.

❝If you have faith, you will have a good time while everybody else is stressed out.

Faith in God will make you a legend.

Faith has everything to do with your interpersonal relationship with God.

You can't have faith without God because your faith has everything to do with God.

Someone dying shouldn't change your faith.

Faith isn't afraid to fight for what belongs to it.

Faith is easy to Jesus and will be easy for you once He develops His faith in you.

Faith not only needs a challenge but thrives when challenged.

Jesus was challenged to the core of His being when it came to His faith.

The secret to faith is being led by the Holy Spirit.

Faith has no fear.

Jesus was anointed to teach faith.

Anyone who is a friend of God will have faith.

Faith is something unique, and not everyone has it.

Faith always has the last laugh.

The more faith you have, the more God can use you.

The secret to strong faith is being able to overcome all opposition and resistance until the Word of God is manifested.

Faith not only believes God can perform a miracle but persistently bugs God until He does.

Faith puts a demand on God to keep His covenant.

Faith makes no room for self-pity but aggressively and thankfully inherits the promises of God.

It's impossible to defeat faith.

Faith is always optimistic and thankful.

Faith never says it is a victim.

Faith keeps believing when all others have given up all hope.

Faith puts a demand on God to fulfill His Word.

Thinking the thoughts of God found in His Word makes you strong in faith.

God is looking for someone He can develop to the point where the whole world marvels and talks about their faith.

Never, never, never speak any thoughts of fear, doubt, and unbelief.

Once you use your faith and receive a miracle from God you are never the same.

Real faith never gives up.

Faith is bold like a lion.

Faith is strong and very courageous.

66 *Overcoming faith needs something to overcome.*

Faith has guts, intestinal fortitude, and a strong backbone.

Anyone strong in faith will be extraordinary.

Faith knows how to believe its way out of a rock and a hard place.

Faith only connects with faith.

Have faith in God and not in your faith.

Your faith must unite with God's faith for faith to work.

Some people think they have strong faith until a fiery trial tests them.

The trial of your faith reveals where your faith is and is also used to perfect it.

Faith will keep speaking to a mountain until it moves.

Mountains don't listen to weak, little, or dead faith.

Faith understands that mountains don't always like to obey.

Death cannot defeat faith.

Nothing can defeat faith.

Faith never gets discouraged.

Faith hunts for and eradicates negative thoughts.

Faith never worries about something it has no control over.

Faith doesn't worry about anything!

Demons only obey Christians with strong faith.

I would rather have great faith than a big ministry.

Faith laughs in the face of impossibilities.

If you want to please God, you must learn everything you can about faith.

Faith is eternal and never quits or gives up.

The devil is only afraid of Christians who are strong in faith.

Faith is not bound by space and time, and it never stops believing God.

Strong faith has the power to force a miracle to happen.

Faith knows that just because there is a delay doesn't mean that God will not keep His Word.

Faith knows how to hang on to God's promises, even if things look bad.

Faith is the language of God; therefore, if you are going to speak to God, you must speak to Him in faith.

God's creative ability is His faith at work.

Faith laughs in the face of danger.

❝Always remember that when you are believing God for a miracle that God is in the same boat with you.

Faith stays joyous during an attack because it knows beyond a shadow of a doubt that God will come through every time.

When a situation goes from bad to worse, faith keeps believing God until victory is achieved.

Faith turns defeat into victory every time.

You will not grow in your God given faith until you see fear, doubt, unbelief, and worry as a sin.

Faith loves a challenge and always arises to the occasion.

Faith always defeats all opposition.

You can't kill faith.

The preaching of faith is the secret to having a revival.

The anointing can only match your level of faith.

Strong faith fights through all opposition and contradiction until it manifests the Word of God.

Real faith understands there is an enemy who will stop at nothing to keep the Word of God from manifesting.

Faith ignores anything and everything that would try to lie and say that God's Word is not true.

If you want to have great faith in God, you must settle into the fact that you will be tested.

Faith only focuses on the truth of God's Word until it manifests.

Faith never backs down from a fight.

When all looks lost, faith keeps going.

Faith is not afraid of opposition or resistance to the Word of God because faith knows that God cannot lie.

Faith will always come out on top at any test thrown at it.

Faith is not afraid of the time it may take God to manifest His Word.

Your inward eye of faith allows you to plainly see the path of God for your life that no one else can see.

Keep your foot on the throttle of your faith, and you will see your prayers answered speedily.

You cannot access the blessings of the kingdom of God without faith.

Faith knows God has answered its prayer and doesn't stop believing, even if things get worse.

Faith is a measure of Spiritual authority and power that God gives through obedience, decreed by spoken words.

We have to use our faith in God to give God the authority to use His faith to help us in our situation.

Faith starts and ends in what is revealed in the scriptures.

If you always live in a low-level state of fear, doubt, and unbelief, you will never come into the powerful potential of living by faith, where miracles and Divine answers to your prayers manifest on a regular basis.

Once you've decided to quit worrying, you've opened yourself up to living by faith.

A guilty conscience will ruin your chance of speaking by faith and getting your prayers answered by God.

You cannot speak to mountains by faith and expect them to move if you doubt God and His Word in your heart.

Patience is vital to faith.

Faith loves to pray for people in terrible conditions and see them healed.

Faith never complains but is always thankful for all things.

❝Faith in God is mental toughness that enables you to believe and muscle your way through adversity and come out on top every time.

You have to learn how to enter into by faith the covenants God made with Abraham, David, and Christ to receive blessings from God.

The prayer of faith can change the world.

You can't be in faith and worry at the same time.

When you have faith, you will always have tangible answers from God Almighty.

Faith will blind you to your problems and open your eyes to only God's answers.

Strict adherence to the Words of Christ creates an unshakeable faith in the believer.

Your faith will leap over all of your limitations once you get a full revelation of God's sovereignty, power, ability, and willingness to help you.

Fear, doubt, worry, and unbelief are the enemies of God.

God cannot stand not being believed in because everything about Him is inherently good, and He has the power to do anything.

Great peace comes upon those who believe and trust in God.

You can miss out on many blessings from God by not believing in Him and what He says.

There is no end to what God will do for those who trust and believe in Him.

Bad news fears men and women of God who walk by faith.

Faith is more than just mere optimism.

Nothing can stop the will of God when you pray the prayer of faith.

Faith breaks through the wall of worry.

The key to real faith is to stay just as excited during the time of testing as when miracles are manifesting.

Your faith needs to be continually exercised to become stronger.

Challenging and contrary situations are opportunities and blessings to exercise and strengthen your faith.

Before you can possess strong faith, all your worries must be dealt with.

Don't expect to have great faith if you are unwilling to do the work of reading, studying, and practicing the Word of God.

Faith can walk through a minefield of fear, doubt, worry, and unbelief and come out unscathed.

Learning to live by faith is more beneficial than a high-paying job.

Worry will put you on the defensive, but faith puts you on the offensive.

Miracles don't just happen on their own; someone has to have faith.

❝Bad news is a test to see if you will back off your faith in God and start worrying.

If you have strong faith in God, you can live like a king or queen while the rest of the world is going through hell.

You can't tackle life problems with little, weak, or dead faith.

The just live by faith and not by random luck.

There is nothing you cannot believe for and nothing you cannot do when you have faith in God.

God will do anything and everything to help a faith-filled man or woman of God.

It's not hoping that things get done but knowing by faith that it is done that gets things done.

You will experience exactly what you believe.

Jesus did not perform any miracles for people where someone was not actively involved with their faith for the miracle to manifest.

If you could see the future that God has for you, you would have more faith in the present.

The only thing that can stop God's power is the lack of faith.

❝ I don't want to hear how much faith you have; I want to see you get out on the battlefield of life and prove how much faith you have.

You cannot turn the world upside down with weak faith.

Faith is the original blueprint, design, and framework by which all of heaven operates.

God wants to get us to the place where we fully believe Him without seeing anything with our naked eye.

The devil is no match against someone who knows the Word of God and is strong in faith.

Faith is not afraid to fight the devil over God's Word being true.

Hebrews 11:6 (KJV)
But without faith it is impossible to please him: for he that cometh to God must believe that he is, and that he is a rewarder of them that diligently seek him.

CHAPTER 13

❖

Fear

❝ Whatever you fear rules you.

God wants you to be feared by your enemies.

God transforms you from being intimidated by the devil to one who intimidates the devil.

God can transform you from being afraid to the one who the enemy fears.

Fear is a byproduct of sin.

A healthy fear of God will keep you from sin.

Fear is a weapon.

Fear is a weapon used by both God and the devil.

Only fear a prophet or prophetess if all of their words come to pass.

The blessing of prophetic insight is it removes the fear of the unknown because you can see what God is doing.

What the world fears about death is a promotion with God for a Christian.

Fearlessness and courage can solve a lot of problems.

If you don't have God in your life, you need to be afraid.

Don't get sucked into the trap of fearful and doubtful thinking.

Fear, doubt, and unbelief are the storms that are on the inside of you, not on the outside.

One of the toughest things to do in life is to face your fears.

Fear is a liar, and you know how I hate lying.

Don't let other people's fear get transferred into your faith-filled mind.

Fear is an invasive force and, if not stood up against and defeated, will take over everything,

Someone could have $1 million in the bank and still be living in fear.

Never fear the retaliation of the devil when you're right with God.

Fear doesn't want things to get worse, but faith doesn't care if things get worse.

As a Christian, you should never fear the curses of a witch or warlock.

When you are fearful, you become a victim of more things than you normally would be.

Fear itself can become a very real threat if you let it.

Fear is a punk and bully who needs to be taken out back and beaten every chance you get.

I am no longer sitting and eating at the table of fear, doubt, and unbelief.

Never speak or operate out of a spirit of fear, doubt, or unbelief.

❝ *Bad news fears me.*

Fear is a thief that steals blessings from God.

Fear will tell you that you don't have an answer from God when you do, but if you believe your fear, you can lose out on that answer.

There is only one way to take on your fears and that is head on.

2 Timothy 1:7 (KJV)
7 For God hath not given us the spirit of fear; but of power, and of love, and of a sound mind.

CHAPTER 14

Forgiveness

❝Having a spirit of forgiveness is like having a wall of protection around your heart and spirit.

God is very giving and forgiving; when you start to give and forgive, you will become more like Him.

A wise person forgives people before they even sin against them.

A weak person takes their time in forgiving someone, while a strong person forgives people before they even commit an offense.

Just because I forgive you doesn't mean I trust you. You have to earn that trust back.

Forgiveness is automatic, but trust has to be earned.

Matthew 18:21-22 (KJV)

21 Then came Peter to him, and said, Lord, how oft shall my brother sin against me, and I forgive him? till seven times? 22 Jesus saith unto him, I say not unto thee, Until seven times: but, Until seventy times seven.

CHAPTER 15

Holy Spirit

❝A lot of people want the anointing; I want the Holy Spirit.

We have the same Holy Spirit that enforced all of the blessings of God on Jesus when He rose Him from the dead.

The Holy Spirit enforces all the blessings of God on us if we will believe in the finished work of Christ.

There is a place in the Spirit where all obstacles seem like wax to fire, and they just easily melt away.

A Christian can be so filled with the Holy Spirit that impossibilities seem like small stepping stones.

All hell shakes in fear at the thought of a man or woman of God coming into their Holy Spirit identity in Christ.

It takes a lot of work and focus to stay continually filled with the Holy Spirit.

The Holy Spirit carries out the will of the Father.

Evangelism is easy when the Holy Spirit is involved.

The Holy Spirit in the life of a New Testament Christian is the image that creates the shadow of the Old Covenant.

Without the Holy Spirit, humanity is only left to operate by the arm of the flesh.

Life is easy when you have the Holy Spirit.

Holy Spirit laughter is the best antidote for this world's problems.

After the fall of Adam, man had to learn how to live without the authority and power of the Holy Spirit.

Once you know what the Ark of the Covenant is, you will understand who the Holy Spirit is.

The Ark of the Covenant was created to represent the Holy Spirit.

We must keep anything and everything out of our lives that hinders the Holy Spirit from manifesting in our lives.

Once the Ark of the Covenant leaves a place, you won't' find any manifestation of the Holy Spirit.

A welcomed Divine Interruption is when the Holy Spirit falls on a person or a place.

Whenever the Holy Spirit falls on a place, everything changes.

As the Ark is to the temple, so is the Holy Spirit to the born-again believer.

One outpouring of the Holy Spirit can fix years of bad theology.

When the Holy Spirit falls, you get filled.

I'm a better person when I am filled with the Holy Spirit.

Lust can drain a man of the Holy Spirit in seconds.

The Holy Spirit is full of emotions; when you are full of the Holy Spirit, so will you.

❝The best thing that can happen to someone's life is to have the Holy Spirit fall on them as on the day of Pentecost.

Wise Christians protect their relationship with the Holy Spirit like Fort Knox protects the gold.

There is a spirit behind everything in this life; if it is not the Holy Spirit, it is a human or unclean spirit.

The Holy Spirit will lead you to the Word, and the Word will lead you to the Holy Spirit.

When the Anointing of the Holy Spirit is on your life, religious and demonic people will want to kill you.

I don't just want to know the Scriptures; I want to know the Holy Spirit who inspired the Scriptures.

You have to get into Gods Word and the Holy Spirit to get the curse of Babel off of you.

The only way to escape the curse of Babel is to be filled with the Holy Spirit.

Flesh is attracted to flesh. Spirit is attracted to Spirit.

Speaking in tongues breaks the curse of Babel off of you.

You can expect great things to happen when you obey God and are led by His Spirit.

You can get to a place in your relationship with the Holy Spirit where you can depend upon Him for anything and everything in your life.

There is a spirit behind every word spoken: a human spirit, an evil spirit, or the Holy Spirit.

Living your life without the Holy Spirit is death.

Individuals are raised up by God for specific tasks and gifted by the Holy Spirit to help them accomplish what God has called them to do.

The only way to successfully make it through this life and enter the Kingdom of God is utter dependence on God the Father, the Lord Jesus Christ, and the precious Holy Spirit.

Your job is to remove all distractions from your life and seek the kingdom of God and His righteousness first. If you do this, God will unlock the secrets of how to walk and live in the Spirit.

You cannot defeat your flesh without the power of the Holy Spirit.

The Holy Spirit is the voice of wisdom.

The Holy Spirit can take better care of you than you can take care of yourself.

The secret to unlocking the Kingdom of God in your life is that you must be led by the Holy Spirit every second, minute, and hour of the day.

The Holy Spirit will lead you into God's Word, will, love, and ways.

It's not just about prayer or reading the Word; you have to be led by the Holy Spirit to get closer to God.

When the Holy Spirit always leads you, you are always in and doing God's will.

The Holy Spirit will never lead you into sin or rebellion against God.

The Holy Spirit will always lead you to a closer walk with God.

You must ask the Holy Spirit to lead you because He will never control you.

The Word God teaches you how to be led by the Spirit.

Confidence comes by continually being led by the Spirit.

❝**When the Holy Spirit leads you, you will always be in the right place, at the right time, and with the right word.**

You can only access the Conversation of the Godhead by being led by the Holy Spirit.

Some people want an extravagant life; I want an extravagant life in the Spirit.

The Holy Spirit is found in the Word of God, and when you get the Word of God in you, the Holy Spirit will be found in you.

You should get so tuned into the voice of the Holy Spirit that He can whisper something to you, and you hear it and do it.

If you take the time to tune into the Holy Spirit, He will give you great ideas in the middle of every situation or problem.

When the Holy Spirit leads you, you are always many steps ahead of the enemy.

When the Holy Spirit leads you, you will look back and see that He worked everything out in your favor way before you even got there.

If you want the spirit of Elijah to come upon you, you better be prepared to die to everything and spend a lot of time alone with God.

If you are going to be led by the Holy Spirit successfully, you will have to master listening to the still small voice.

The secret to living a victorious Christian life is to learn how to be continually led by the Holy Spirit.

The world can come crashing down on you if the Holy Spirit does not lead you.

I don't have to know everything; I have to know the Holy Spirit because He knows everything and will tell me what I need to know in advance and when I need to know it.

The Holy Spirit has the most powerful yet softest voice many people never hear.

Acts 1:8 (KJV)
8 But ye shall receive power, after that the Holy Ghost is come upon you: and ye shall be witnesses unto me both in Jerusalem, and in all Judaea, and in Samaria, and unto the uttermost part of the earth.

CHAPTER 16

Image of God

❝You have to be imprinted with God's image for what you are called to do before you can do what God has called you to do.

Your name has a lot to do with the imprint of the image of God on your life.

God will change your name if your name doesn't fit the image of who you are called to be.

The Holy Spirit continually challenges us to come into the full image of the Son of God.

Changing into the image of Christ will be painful because you will have to die to yourself to do it.

The Lord is only with His sons who are bearing His image.

The express image of the Father is encoded in the Words of Christ.

You cannot build the image of Christ within you if you have too many distractions.

Maturing the internal and eternal image of God within you is the most important thing you need to work on in this life.

I am not called to be conformed to the image of who you think I should be, but who God says I am.

Everything you think, say, and do flows from your inward image of who you are.

Changing into the image of Christ will take a lot of study of the Word of God and much prayerful meditation.

Everything in your life is dictated by the inward image of who you are.

The image of God has to be built into your mindset and how you think about yourself in every area of your life.

Going from glory to glory and being transformed into the image of Christ is inwardly painful.

To be transformed into the image of Christ, something has to die.

You have to have the Holy Spirit engrained into the image of who you are for the anointing to work in your life.

If your dad is not a son of God, God will disconnect you from him when you become a son of God.

No one has a right to talk into your identity but God.

Never let anyone speak into your identity because only God knows who you are called to be.

You have to inwardly become what God wants you to outwardly manifest.

Your thoughts, words, and actions must catch up to the image God placed inside of you at the new birth.

The Kingdom of God is not just a place; it is characteristics of the image of God that you become.

Who you used to be does not have to dictate who you can become in God.

God shows you your future self to your present self so you can look back and see you were shown who to be.

You have to follow the path of God's thoughts to get to higher levels of living in the image of God.

❝It's not who you've been in your past that matters, but who you end up becoming.

You cannot come into who you are to become in God if you are not willing to admit and change who you presently are.

Never let a family member tear down the image of God in you.

The only way to become more like the image of Christ is to look at Him, and I mean really look at Him.

When God changes you into His image, you must quit thinking about who you used to be and focus on the new you.

Thinking about who you used to be can hinder the process of you becoming more like God.

God sees who you can and will become before you do.

Until you get to where you can stand alone with the Lord, you will never fully realize who and what you are called to be.

If you practice and think about the Word of God long enough, at some point, you are imprinted and changed into the Words you are obeying.

The only opinion that should matter to you about who you are is God's.

2 Corinthians 4:3-4 (KJV)

3 But if our gospel be hid, it is hid to them that are lost: 4 In whom the god of this world hath blinded the minds of them which believe not, lest the light of the glorious gospel of Christ, who is the image of God, should shine unto them.

CHAPTER 17

✦

Imagination

❝You are limited to how you see yourself within yourself in your imagination.

A promise from the Word of God is God's imagination for you.

Reality, as we know it in the world we see, dwells inside the virtual imagination of God.

Nothing you imagine to do will be impossible.

Your imagination is your internal eyes that allow you to see within yourself things that have happened, are happening, will happen, or can happen.

Your imagination doesn't know the difference between what it sees if it has happened or will happen. Your imagination is eternal and operates outside of time.

Your imagination gives your Faith something to believe God for.

The promises from the Word of God are given to paint images in your heart that give you hope. Your faith takes these imprinted images of hope from your imagination and speaks them into existence through the power of the Holy Spirit.

The Holy Spirit wrote the Word of God. The Word of God is filled with precious promises that paints a picture of hope in your imagination.

Your words of faith activate the Holy Spirit to perform what you are hoping for in your imagination.

You have to take the Sword of God's Word and go to battle with your evil imagination.

Your imagination has the power to see and create future events by the Word of God.

Your imagination has the ability to in the unseen world and invisible God.

Your imagination has the ability to see you doing evil before you sin and doing righteousness.

You operate and function in the world out of the image that you see yourself to be.

The devil knows the power of your imagination and will implant imaginations in your heart that are against the will of God for your life, and if you don't cast them down, they will come to pass.

Genesis 11:6 (KJV)

And the Lord said, Behold, the people is one, and they have all one language; and this they begin to do: and now nothing will be restrained from them, which they have imagined to do.

CHAPTER 18

※

Knowing God

❝You have to listen to the still small voice of the Spirit daily if you want to know God.

Most Christians barely scratch the surface of really knowing God.

You can only come to know God by spending years in prayer and study of His Word as He reveals Himself to you.

You can judge me all you want, but I am living a secret life with God that I don't want you to know about, and that's been going on for years.

Just because you know about God doesn't mean you know Him.

The grandest benefit of Christianity is getting the opportunity to know God on a personal level.

There is nothing, absolutely nothing, more precious in this life than having a genuine walk with God.

It's not just what you know about God that matters, but what you live and obey from His Word.

I ask, seek, and knock to know God.

Some people want big ministries: I want a BIG relationship with God.

You have to live a disciplined life to stay right with God.

The more profound revelations of the kingdom of God are hidden behind deeper commitments to God.

I would rather have God as my friend than a million other friends.

God is better to me than a million friends put together.

If you are going to get closer to God, you are going to have to make some deep decisions in your heart about death to your flesh.

Many people know their Bible, but very few know God.

It is very hard to get to know God, and not for the faint of heart.

Some ministers know a lot about God but don't really know Him.

To grow and get closer to God, you must disconnect from your flesh and all of its cravings.

You must make spiritual higher ground daily to get closer to God and become who He has called you to be.

The closer you get to God, the more gracious you will hear Him speak to you.

Prophetic insight into the future gives you Divine peace no matter what you are going through, and you only get this insight through a close walk with God.

To be close to God, you must do anything He asks you to do.

❝It will cost you everything if you want to get to know God.

You will never get into heaven on the merits of working miracles, prophesying, or casting out demons. The only way to get into heaven is by knowing God and doing His will.

Not everyone who does miracles, signs, and wonders knows God.

My relationship with God has developed little by little as I have read, studied, prayed, and understood who He is.

1 John 4:7-8 (KJV)
*7 Beloved, let us love one another: for love is of God;
and every one that loveth is born of God, and knoweth
God. 8 He that loveth not knoweth not God;
for God is love.*

CHAPTER 19

Lust

66 **All lust is a temptation to see if you will be unfaithful to God.**

Lust is the enemy of faithfulness as it tries to seduce people to give up their eternal Covenant with God for temporary pleasure.

The highest form of the lust of the flesh is sex.

Lust makes it where you want to see what you are not supposed to look at.

Lust will try to cause you to forsake everything you believe in and stand for.

Lust will leave you desperately poor.

1 John 2:15-17 (KJV)
15 Love not the world, neither the things that are in the world. If any man love the world, the love of the Father is not in him. 16 For all that is in the world, the lust of the flesh, and the lust of the eyes, and the pride of life, is not of the Father, but is of the world. 17 And the world passeth away, and the lust thereof: but he that doeth the will of God abideth for ever.

CHAPTER 20

⊰❈⊱

Martyrdom

❝The ultimate way to prove your love to God is to be willing to die for Him.

A Christian who loves God with all their heart will have no problem laying down their life to prove that love to Him.

The only way to prove your pure motives of loving a God who is all-powerful is to be willing to lay down the life He gave you.

Face being a martyr for Christ like a hero.

The early Christians proved their love for God by dying for Him.

It would be the highest honor to die for Christ.

Death to yourself, your flesh, and actual death for being a Christian is the highest forms of showing your love towards God.

Don't think you are going to raise the dead if you are not willing to die for Christ.

Revelation 12:11 (KJV)
And they overcame him by the blood of the Lamb, and by the word of their testimony; and they loved not their lives unto the death.

CHAPTER 21

❧

Meditation

❝ There are some places in God and the Spirit you cannot reach without deep meditation.

Decision-making meditation in the Holy Spirit will change your life forever.

You will have to do a lot of Holy Ghost meditation if you want to go far in your walk with God.

Deep meditation on the Word of God generates Divine questions and answers.

Meditation on the Word of God allows you to penetrate the deep thoughts of God.

1 Timothy 4:15 (KJV)
Meditate upon these things; give thyself wholly to them; that thy profiting may appear to all.

CHAPTER 22

✦❖✦

Mind Renewal

❝An unrenewed mind doesn't' read the Bible the same way a renewed mind reads the Bible.

An unrenewed mind reads things into the Bible that are not there.

It's doctrines of demons and unbiblical ways of thinking that keep you from operating in the power of God and as a son of God.

An unrenewed mind comes up with false teachings and doctrines from the Word of God.

Romans 12:2 (KJV)
2 And be not conformed to this world: but be ye transformed by the renewing of your mind, that ye may prove what is that good, and acceptable, and perfect, will of God.

CHAPTER 23

Ministry

❝ Who you become in God will ultimately determine the ministry God can use you for.

Some of the most powerful ministries take 30, 40, 50, and up to 80 years to prepare for and may only last 3 years.

God puts into the ministry those He trusts because they are faithful.

God wouldn't put us through all this without putting us into the ministry.

The more powerful the ministry you are called to, the more powerful the person you must become.

Don't think you have to get married to be successful in ministry; you might be better off being single.

You have to become the person who can carry the ministry you are called to.

It takes years and years of training to prepare you for what God has prepared you to do.

A man or woman who doesn't know or repented of their wretchedness isn't a good minister of Jesus Christ.

A man or woman of God who has fallen and gotten back up has a deeper compassion for those they are ministering to.

Giving is a wonderful and powerful thing that a minister should never exploit.

Intercessory ministries are like a snipers because they can take out an enemy on the other side of the planet or in another realm.

1 Timothy 1:12 (KJV)
And I thank Christ Jesus our Lord, who hath enabled me, for that he counted me faithful, putting me into the ministry;

CHAPTER 24

Miracles

"Don't let the devil think you are crazy for believing God for miracles, speaking to mountains, and calling those things that be not as though they were.

The great thing about having God on your side is that He can make a miracle come out of nowhere and save the day.

Miracles alter the course of history.

Every time God does a miracle, it reveals His glory.

The devil always laughs at people until God does a miracle and gives you the last laugh.

Every time God does a miracle, His glory is revealed.

God is glorified whenever He displays His power through a miracle.

We have to believe God for miracles and not because of miracles.

If you are not getting blown away by miracles, you're not seeing the kingdom of God.

The Gospel is the Good News that God will perform powerful miracles.

One miracle the devil cannot duplicate is the raising of the dead.

Don't ever try to bypass the hard work it takes to get a miracle from God by cheap tricks and faithless workarounds.

It is exciting to see what miracle God is going to do next.

God has to give you the thoughts He thinks for you to have a miracle mindset.

Your mind has to be strong enough to withstand the battle for a miracle to occur.

There is always an enemy you have to defeat before any miracle can occur.

When you hear God at a deeper level, you will begin to see miracles take place in accordance with His Divine will in Heaven.

You have to be powerful on the inside to produce powerful miracles on the outside.

Don't let setbacks or bad news discourage you when believing God for a miracle.

God loves to do miracles when someone believes.

It takes a miracle-thinking mindset to create miracles.

Most people are stressed out until a miracle happens because they don't have faith in God.

You can't do the miracles Jesus did unless you have the faith Jesus has.

"God will start doing miracles when He can find a believer strong enough to withstand all the attacks that come with them.

You have to receive miracles before you work miracles.

I live in the land of miracles, where anything and everything is possible.

Galatians 3:5 (KJV)
He therefore that ministereth to you the Spirit, and worketh miracles among you, doeth he it by the works of the law, or by the hearing of faith?

CHAPTER 25

Obedience

❝God wants to spoil you, if you could just be mature enough to obey Him.

You can count on God to bless you if you obey Him.

God will give you an answer to all of your problems if you obey Him.

The more you obey God, the more you fall in love with Him.

You can teach grace all you want but it still doesn't deny the fact that you have to obey all of the commands of Christ to be right with God.

You must love obeying God if you want to be close to Him and get anywhere with Him in your life.

Everything in your walk with God is hinging upon your obedience to God.

The more you fall in love with God, the more you obey Him.

You can't blame others for bringing a curse on yourself because of your own disobedience.

There are heavy consequences for disobedience.

Always obey what God told you to do for yourself and not what someone else said God said for you to do.

Acts 5:32 (KJV)
And we are his witnesses of these things; and so is also the Holy Ghost, whom God hath given to them that obey him.

CHAPTER 26

Power of God

66 Incorrect ways of believing, thinking, and acting affect your faith, which affects the power of God from flowing through you.

The power of God works through a believer with a mind that has been accurately renewed by the Word of God.

The power of God works more off revelations from the word of God, which increases your faith and not feelings.

False doctrines, and wrong and incorrect ways of thinking stop the power of God from working through you.

The power of God works best in a Christian with a renewed mind.

The knowledge of God unlocks the power of God operating in your life through a renewed mind.

The knowledge of God revealed in His Word affects your faith, and it is your faith that enables you to minister with the power of God.

Romans 1:16 (KJV)

For I am not ashamed of the gospel of Christ: for it is the power of God unto salvation to every one that believeth; to the Jew first, and also to the Greek.

CHAPTER 27

✦

Prayer

❝God doesn't just answer prayers; He answers prayers of faith.

Answers to your prayers were created before God made the world; you just have to believe for them to come to pass.

It takes a lot of warfare to birth answers to prayers.

As Christians, we are built to pray just like an eagle is built to fly in the sky.

If you disobey God's laws or violate your conscience, you lose your spiritual authority, thereby stopping your ability to decree and make things come to pass in prayer.

The best practice while waiting for an answer from God in prayer is to be thankful.

You have to build such a trusting relationship with God that you know He will answer your prayers despite what you see.

God ordains and sets up answers to your prayers way before you even ask, but your faith causes it to come to pass.

Some people get excited only when they see an answer to their prayer; I get excited when I know God heard me before the answers come because I know God is going to do it.

The more you listen to God and do what He says, the more He will listen to you and do what you ask when you pray.

If God heard your prayer and it lines up with His will you have the answer to your prayer.

Once you know God heard your prayer, begin to speak to the mountain.

Mark 11:23-24 (KJV)

23 For verily I say unto you, That whosoever shall say unto this mountain, Be thou removed, and be thou cast into the sea; and shall not doubt in his heart, but shall believe that those things which he saith shall come to pass; he shall have whatsoever he saith. 24 Therefore I say unto you, What things soever ye desire, when ye pray, believe that ye receive them, and ye shall have them.

CHAPTER 28

Prophets

❝Study everything that a false prophet does, don't do any of it and you won't be one.

If you do not want to be right with God, stay away from the prophets because they will nail you.

Don't marry Jezebel, live like Ahab, and expect Elijah the prophet to be happy with you.

The greater the evil, the stronger the prophet God has to raise up.

Prosperity is found in the prophetic Word of God spoken by the prophets of the Lord.

There are more false pastors than there are false prophets.

Matthew 7:15-16 (KJV)
15 Beware of false prophets, which come to you in sheep's clothing, but inwardly they are ravening wolves. 16 Ye shall know them by their fruits. Do men gather grapes of thorns, or figs of thistles?

CHAPTER 29

◆

Quotes

❝Great quotes can pack a lot of power in the time of need.

A perfectly timed quote from God can defeat years of demonic mind control and senseless thoughts of the devil.

A high-powered thought or quote from God is like a devastating weapon against your enemy.

Quotes have more impact coming from the life of a person who demonstrated and came up with the quote.

You can draw a lot of strength and wisdom from a great quote.

Quotes are only good if you put them to use in your life.

It's a good idea that you get in a habit of quickly writing down any quote God gives you so you don't lose it.

A quote is like a whole sermon in and of itself.

I hate losing a great quote because I didn't write it down when it came to me.

A quote is only helpful if you put it to good use.

I didn't make these quotes up; God gave them to me through years of serving Him.

Powerful quotes are birthed out of a life of someone who lives and studies the Word of God.

You can learn a lot about a person by the quotes they come up with or think about on a regular basis.

I don't just make these quotes up; I live by them.

You will find many powerful quotes in the minds of everyone who did anything great.

Powerful quotes belong to powerful people, and weak quotes belong to weak people.

History is filled with remarkable people who lived and died by the quotes they believed in.

Show me someone who did something great in this life and I will show you a person who lived by or came up with many powerful quotes!

The Bible is filled with powerful quotes that we are called to live by, think about, and speak all day long.

Jesus spoke the most powerful quotes ever.

God uses powerful quotes to strengthen His people in a time of great need.

The mysteries of God's kingdom are hidden in parables and powerful quotes.

It's amazing how a small one-liner quote can change the world.

It doesn't matter who came up with the quote; what matters if you have the strength or wisdom of the quote to use in your time of need.

I dare you to write down, study, and think about powerful quotes on a regular basis and see what happens to your life.

The devil hates and fears believers who live by powerful quotes.

66 Victory for most people is just a few quotes away.

Powerful quotes are like an unbreakable mind defense by those who think about and live by them.

An ordinary man can become extraordinary once he is filled with and prepared to live by great quotes.

Men and women live and die by the quotes they think about on a regular basis.

The greater the quotes a person thinks about, the more success that person will have in his life.

Not every quote is on the same level of impact, so choose wisely the ones you write down and think about.

Songs are filled with quotes, so be careful what music you listen to.

The world is ruled by quotes more than we realize, so we must create and live by powerful quotes to change the world.

A good beat to a song can carry a devastating thought or quote from the devil, so be careful.

Never underestimate the effect a powerful quote can have on someone's life.

Sometimes, all it takes is one impactful quote delivered at the right time to alter someone's destiny.

Study famous people's lives, what they did, and the quotes that they lived by.

Behind every legend is a stack of extraordinary and powerful quotes.

Every legend has used powerful quotes to stand on to get them to the next level as they climb to the highest peaks of the mountain of life.

You are only as great as the thoughts and quotes you live by.

The enemy fears an army filled with powerful quotes.

❝❝Show me any man or woman who did anything great throughout history and I will show you a person that is filled with great and powerful quotes.

If you gather a collection of quotes and meditate on them, they can have a huge effect on who you become as a person.

Once you start becoming the quotes you are reading or coming up with, you are ready to start changing the world.

Proverbs 1:6 (KJV)

To understand a proverb, and the interpretation; the words of the wise, and their dark sayings.

CHAPTER 30

⋇

Reality

❝Real reality is based upon what God says and not what you actually see, hear or touch.

The reality is that God can change reality.

I don't know the reality you are living in, but I choose to live in the one that God spoke and speaks into existence.

Your words have the power to take a thought and turn it into a reality.

The reality is that you don't have what it takes; you have to find in God what it takes for you to overcome in this life.

2 Corinthians 4:18 (KJV)
While we look not at the things which are seen, but at the things which are not seen: for the things which are seen are temporal; but the things which are not seen are eternal.

CHAPTER 31

❧

Revelations

❝People will think you are a heretic when you reveal revelations that are beyond where they are at.

Revelation always proceeds manifestation.

You have to understand the revelations of God in your heart before you can speak them with your mouth.

There are Divine revelations at the places of Divine locations.

If you are not willing to live in the dedication of a revelation that is given to you, don't ask for it, because you will be held accountable for it.

Every revelation from God has a requirement connected to it.

Knowledge leads to inspiration, then to revelation, then to dedication, then to transformation, and finally to manifestation.

Ephesians 1:18 (KJV)
The eyes of your understanding being enlightened;
that ye may know what is the hope of his calling, and
what the riches of the glory of his inheritance in the
saints,

CHAPTER 32

⸎

Sin

❝All sin is the breaking of covenant with God.

All sin has to be either forgiven or judged.

When Jesus died on the cross He not only paid the price for your sins, but He also freed you from the power of sin so you won't sin anymore.

The price tag on sin is very expensive. You really can't afford it.

You cannot break the cycle of the curse through positive thinking if you are still living in sin.

If you are living in sin, you will have no power with God.

The best thing that could happen to you is to hear from God and Him calling you to repentance if you were sinning. When He's silent, you need to be worried.

When it gets right down to it, Christianity is about you repenting of your sins and becoming faithful to God.

You lose access to God when you sin unless you repent.

The shed blood of Jesus Christ purges and cleanses away the sin of a repentant Christian.

When you sin, you set back the development and formation of the image of God within you.

One little unrepented sin can affect your eternal destiny.

The fastest way to get restored when you sin is to be honest with yourself, admit you were wrong to God, change your ways, and ask God to forgive you.

Sin will make you an immature Christian, set you back, and keep you from all the blessings of God.

Sin will dwarf your spiritual growth.

There are heavy consequences that come with sin and disobedience that make it just not worth the price to go down that road.

Romans 6:1-3 (KJV)
1 What shall we say then? Shall we continue in sin, that grace may abound? 2 God forbid. How shall we, that are dead to sin, live any longer therein? 3 Know ye not, that so many of us as were baptized into Jesus Christ were baptized into his death?

CHAPTER 33

·❖·

Sons of God

❝I'm no longer just a human. I'm a son of God.

A wise son of God has the authority and power to handle any situation that comes their way.

God doesn't want his sons to just have authority and power; He wants them to be authority and power.

A privilege of being a son of God is you get to be led by the Holy Spirit.

There is nothing impossible to a son of God.

Nothing is impossible to a wise and powerful son of God who is led by the Holy Spirit.

No man can stand before a son of God.

Every son of God is a sun of righteousness.

You have to believe in the Son of God to become a son of God.

It takes a strong born-again son God to defeat a fallen son of God.

The only way to see and enter the kingdom of God is to be a born-again son of God who is in full right standing with the Father.

A true son of God would never choose a relationship with a woman over God.

God cannot use you the way He wants to until you see yourself as a wise son of God.

When you get chastened by God, be thankful because it proves you are a son of God.

You will have to carry your cross daily to be a son of God.

One of the rites of passage to become a son of God is the death of the flesh.

It's is not easy being a son of God, nor is it for the faint of heart.

Being a son of God will cost you everything.

Jesus became a man so we could become a son of God.

The glorious liberty of being a son of God is death to the lust of the flesh, the lust of the eyes, and the pride of life.

John 1:12 (KJV)
**But as many as received him, to them gave he power
to become the sons of God, even to them that believe
on his name:**

CHAPTER 34

***

Tongues

❝The amount of time you put forth in prayer to administer the Holy Spirit through speaking in tongues is the measure he will work through you and for you.

You can accomplish amazing things when you speak in tongues.

Daily speaking in tongues as much as possible will make a massive difference in your life.

Speaking in tongues will give you a huge advantage over any problem or enemy you are facing.

Speaking in tongues must be an integral part of every believer's life.

1 Corinthians 14:18 (KJV)
I thank my God, I speak with tongues more than ye all:

CHAPTER 35

❈

Strong in the Lord

❝ Most people complain about the very test that they should be thanking God for because it has the potential to make them stronger.

The closer you get to God, the stronger you are at saying no to sin and distractions, and the stronger you are at saying no to sin and distractions, the closer you get to God.

Be strong in the Lord in everything you do.

You must eradicate all levels of weak thinking from your mind to be strong in the Lord.

God doesn't just want you strong; He wants you strong in the Lord and the power of His might.

If you depend only on your own strength, you can never truly become strong in the Lord.

The very fact you don't quit in a trial makes you stronger. Even if you fail get back up quickly and stay in the fight and this will prove you are strong.

Strong people always get back up and learn from their mistakes.

With age and maturity comes strength.

If it were easy, you wouldn't get stronger.

Lust can drain a man of God of his strength like nothing else. *Why are you complaining about the things God is trying to use to make you a stronger man or woman of God?*

To truly get strong, you will have to start liking adversity because you see the value in it.

If you truly want to get stronger, you will have a feast when adversity comes.

Confidence comes from getting back up over and over again until you stand strong in the Lord.

I am strong IN the Lord, not just strong.

For the church to be strong in the Lord, it cannot tolerate sin, the devil, division, or the spirit of Jezebel.

Your past failures can become a big part of a strong foundation if you just don't quit.

You have to learn to be strong at trusting in the Lord.

Lust can utterly weaken and destroy a very strong and powerful man.

Being strong takes a lot of prayer and dependency on the Lord.

Strong Christians read and study their Bible a lot.

It really boils down to you making a choice to be strong in the Lord.

Learn from your mistakes; don't dwell on them because that will only weaken you.

You can emerge triumphant from any battle you face if you are strong and have faith in God.

❝Inward strength comes from mental and inward daily decisions you make to think and be strong.

Jesus will expose all of your weak, fearful, and faithless thoughts in the middle of the trial you are facing if you have any.

The inner voice of the Holy Spirit will always lead you to inner strength and power.

Meditating on your past failures can weaken you in the moment and in the future.

There is no end to how strong in the Lord you can become if you let Him do His perfect work in you.

It takes a lot of prayer and studying the Word of God to get strong in the Lord.

Inner strength comes from daily decisions to be strong in the Lord.

Every time you listen and obey the inner voice of the Holy Spirit, you get stronger and stronger.

Thinking about your past failures with regret will only weaken you. Learning from your past failures will strengthen you.

The Lord can work with strength, faith, and boldness. He can't work with fear, doubt and inner weakness and for that matter who can?

When you make the choice to be strong in the Lord, you will feel the power of that choice surge through your whole being.

If you want the strength of the Lord to surge through every part of your being, then make sure you obey the leading of the Holy Spirit when He speaks to you.

Never fear adversity but rather choose to take on adversity with boldness and strength.

Just keep filling your mind with verses, quotes, and thoughts of strength, and eventually you will become strong.

If you genuinely desire to become strong in the Lord, don't hang out with weak-minded people.

You have to be stronger than the devil you are casting out.

There really is no limit to how strong you can become in the Lord.

The more you say no to lust, the stronger you become.

Too much luxury can weaken you.

If you value being strong in the Lord, you will stay away from all lust.

The Holy Spirit broods on people who choose to be strong in the Lord.

When you go through an intense battle of the mind and you feel weak, if you decide to be strong, you will be filled with strength and feel it.

The stronger you become, the easier it is to win battles, conquer through trials, and overcome temptations.

It takes a lot of work and guts to be a strong Christian.

Lusting after women with your eyes will weaken you.

The stronger you become, the easier tougher situations become for you to lift yourself through.

It takes strength to come against thoughts that don't align with God's Word.

The devil wants to steal your inner strength and relationship with God.

You may have to arise out of a failure before you can enter into that deep inner strength from the Lord.

66 **Being strong in the Lord entails mastery over your thought life, a determined will, and control over your emotions.**

Sometimes, it takes a failure for you to realize that your strength comes only from the Lord fully.

Sometimes, it takes a failure before you move from fake strength to real strength.

You have to be strong enough to withstand the forces of reality to believe God with your faith until it bends to His will.

Most people are not strong enough in their faith to believe God for a miracle because a miracle has to alter the known foundations of reality.

When you make a decision to be strong in the Lord, it's the decision itself that becomes a powerful force within you.

How strong you want to become in the Lord is up to you.

It took me some time to figure this out, but strength comes from a choice you make within yourself, which can get stronger and stronger over time.

The battle to change reality to line up with the will of God is a fight that only the strong can accomplish.

When you sin and violate your conscience it takes time to restore you back to full inner strength.

You must step up into the strength of God that He has called you to walk into.

I am interdependent upon the inner strength of the Holy Spirit.

Through the help of the Holy Spirit, you have to find every hidden thought of weakness in your heart and mind and eradicate it.

Someone who wants to stay weak will always think all discipline is abuse.

Unforgiveness weakens the believer.

Complainers are weak, and weak people complain.

Sin weakens you on the inside.

No one respects a weak person.

There is no arrogance, boasting or pride found in being strong in the Lord.

The things you must be strong about in the Lord also make you strong.

Things get easier to deal with the day you decide to be strong in the Lord.

You can become a very strong and powerful man or woman in God if you will submit to the process.

This is no time to be double-minded and weak in spirit.

To remain strong in the Lord you have to continually stay in the Word and prayer reminding yourself of everything God has taught you.

Righteousness is stronger than evil.

The Armor and weaponry of God is only as powerfully deployed by the strength of the warrior wearing it.

❝ When you preach a weak Gospel, you produce weak Christians.

Life is easier when you live strong in the Lord.

You know you have true strength when you can stand alone.

You must be mentally tougher and stronger than the enemy you are trying to defeat.

God wants you so strong in the Spirit that you become bad news to bad news.

You don't know how strong you are during good times; you find out how strong you are during tough times.

When you become strong in the Lord, don't think that God is going to let all of that strength go to waste.

If you want to be powerful, then think powerful thoughts.

Always choose spiritual strength before physical strength when going into war.

If you listen to weak people, then you will be a weak person.

Weak people listen to weak people, and strong people listen to strong people.

To enter your destiny, you must search out, find, and destroy every trace of mental weakness.

Don't pray for it to be easier, pray for you to be stronger.

Thinking about the failures of your past and looking back will only weaken you.

Witches and warlocks fear strong anointed Christians.

Loving luxury weakens you.

It takes strength to find answers from God.

When God gives you strength, don't give it away to women.

Proverbs 24:10 (KJV)
If thou faint in the day of adversity, thy strength is small.

CHAPTER 36

※

Testing & Trials

❝God wants to know if you are ALL IN ALL THE TIME and that you can be tested by trial by fire.

You have to be tested and pass before you can enter into the next level God has for you.

God will keep you in a holding pattern until you pass the test.

No one is above being tested or tempted.

Being tested over and over again is a big part of the Christian life.

You have to pass your test in your garden and defeat the devil before you can begin to enter into your eternal inheritance.

You cannot enter into other people's tests and help them until you pass your own tests.

Some of your greatest treasures in life are found in your trials that you have gone through.

You cannot pass a test until you face the fact the test is not going away until you pass it.

Some of your greatest attacks and temptations you will face in life come right before God is about to bring you into your destiny.

To change your inner image, it has to be spoken into you by God, and then what is spoken into you must be tested to prove that the change in your inner image has occurred.

Spiritual laziness will rob you of the strength God needs to give you to pass a test, trial or overcome a temptation.

Time tests all people.

Tests don't last forever, so remember that when you are in your darkest moment, think about what you want your testimony to be when the test is over.

Loneliness can drive someone to be tempted to do things they wouldn't normally do.

One of the biggest tests that Jesus was tested with was what He would do when He was isolated from everyone when He was tempted in the dessert.

You can learn a lot about a man by how he holds up under criticism, crisis, opposition, times of testing, and pressure.

When you are being tested, God wants to see how you are going to respond to the thoughts of the devil.

What Elisha revealed to get the mantle of Elijah revealed what it would take to walk in the mantle of Elijah.

Don't test the Lord when you are being tested.

Never let a trial or test go to waste, always pull out of it something from the Lord.

Patience is only proven in a test.

When you pass a test it builds your confidence to believe in all that God has called you to be.

Trials are opportunities to show who you are.

The Lord will put you thru a test so you can see what is in your heart good and bad.

If evil is found in you in the test repent and gain wisdom from what you went thru.

❝❞ Great times of testing lay the foundation of your future walk with God.

Tests reveal to God and yourself where you are and how far you've grown.

It is easy to look in the Bible and judge others for what they did wrong in their time of testing until you go thru a test and make the same mistake.

Wisdom is always found in every test or trial you go through.

You gain more confidence in your walk with God every time you pass a test.

Never judge someone going through a trial or tests.

Job 23:10 (KJV)
But he knoweth the way that I take: when he hath tried me, I shall come forth as gold.

CHAPTER 37

Thoughts

66If you don't want something to happen, don't think about it happening, and definitely don't talk about it.

Don't think like a natural man; you are a son of God.

Something inside me dances and sings just thinking about God.

What if you went into every situation as if you already had the answer? How would you think and act?

If you want to be tough, keep thinking tough thoughts.

The funny thing is, the less you care what people think about you, the more they will respect you.

Some people are trapped by their own negative thinking and speaking and don't even know it.

I could care less about what you think unless you are thinking the thoughts of God.

You have to protect Divine thoughts so you don't lose them.

God loves it when His children start thinking and speaking His thoughts.

There is power in the way God thinks.

Just because you have a thought of doubt doesn't mean you have to speak it.

God is a powerful thinker.

2 Corinthians 10:3-6 (KJV)

3 For though we walk in the flesh, we do not war after the flesh: 4 (For the weapons of our warfare are not carnal, but mighty through God to the pulling down of strong holds;) 5 Casting down imaginations, and every high thing that exalteth itself against the knowledge of God, and bringing into captivity every thought to the obedience of Christ; 6 And having in a readiness to revenge all disobedience, when your obedience is fulfilled.

CHAPTER 38

✦

Upper Hand

❝ You will always have the upper hand when you remain obedient and faithful to God.

A mature Christian who understands his authority in God has the upper hand over the devil.

Strength, maturity, power, authority, knowledge, and determination will give you the upper hand in any battle or situation.

Whoever has God with them and on their side has the upper hand.

Keeping a clean conscience before God will always give you a spiritual, emotional, mental, and legal upper hand.

Knowing the future gives you an upper hand.

Being prepared at all times, with continual learning and training, will give you the upper hand against the enemy.

God always wants His people to have the upper hand.

The Anointing will always give you the upper hand over the enemy.

2 Corinthians 2:14 (KJV)
Now thanks be unto God, which always causeth us to triumph in Christ, and maketh manifest the savour of his knowledge by us in every place.

CHAPTER 39

***

Warfare

❝Prepare yourself for war because, trust me, it's coming.

It has always been God's intention that His people be warriors.

Many Christians don't fully understand they are a warrior engaged in a battle.

The attack brings the blessing.

A hardened warrior thrives with adversity.

Hard workers make for great warriors.

You can tell a lot about a true warrior by his work ethic.

A big part of the attack of the enemy is to make you feel stupid for preparing for the coming war.

Don't go to war with the Ark of the Covenant unless you are obeying the Ten Commandments, because you will just lose and the Ark will be stolen from you.

Don't expect to be able to fight and win your spiritual wars if your heart is not right with God.

Just because you are wearing the Armor of God doesn't mean you have the heart and spirit of an elite warrior, that has to be developed.

The enemy is the devil, the battlefield is your mind, and the objective is to bend reality to the will of God.

Ephesians 6:11-12 (KJV)
11 Put on the whole armour of God, that ye may be able to stand against the wiles of the devil. 12 For we wrestle not against flesh and blood, but against principalities, against powers, against the rulers of the darkness of this world, against spiritual wickedness in high places.

CHAPTER 40

※

Will of God

❝In this life, doing the will of God is more important than anything else you do.

Unforgiveness will throw you out of the will of God.

The will of God is not something you just do, but it is something you become.

Don't just marry to marry. Only marry someone if God really brought you both together and you know beyond a shadow of a doubt that it is the will of God.

If I know something is Gods will I will never quit.

Very few people become the perfect will of God.

1 Thessalonians 5:18 (KJV)
In every thing give thanks: for this is the will of God in Christ Jesus concerning you.

CHAPTER 41

Wisdom of God

❝It's astounding to see how many people don't walk in the wisdom of God considering how they will be accountable to God for their foolish decisions in this life without the ability to go back and make different decisions once they die.

The wisdom of Christ is far greater than the wisdom of Solomon.

The benefits of walking in the wisdom of God are far greater than all of the gold, silver, and precious gems in the world.

Wisdom makes you strong because it keeps you from doing stupid things that weaken you.

It takes a lot of strength to walk in the wisdom of God.

The wisdom of God will make you stronger than any mere man.

There is nothing more valuable than listening to the eternal Divine wisdom of God.

If you see yourself as a wise man or woman of God, you will quit acting like a fool.

Never corrupt your wisdom by acting foolishly.

The fear of the Lord is the beginning of wisdom, and the end of it is loving the Lord your God with all of your heart, mind, body, spirit, soul, and strength.

Shutting your ears to the Divine wisdom of God is the stupidest thing you could ever do in this life.

A wise person is stronger than a whole army.

One wise person can defeat an army of fools.

One wise person can take out a whole army.

Walking as a wise person can earn you the right to walk in the courts of heaven.

Wisdom is more valuable than all the money, gold, and silver in the entire world.

Wise people are the wealthiest people on the planet.

People will travel across the world to hear the wisdom of God being spoken by a man of God.

Wisdom is more valuable than anything else in this world.

The wiser you get, the less you talk and the more you listen.

The wiser you get, the more people will want to listen to you.

All true wisdom comes from the Father, Son, and Holy Spirit.

One of the quickest ways to get God to honor you is to receive all the wisdom that comes from out of His mouth.

Acting like a fool is a dishonor to your maker.

66 The wisest thing you can do is read, listen, obey, and teach all of the Words of Christ.

True wealth is building the image of the wisdom of God inside of your heart, mind, soul, and spirit.

If you want to build the image of a wise person within you, you will have to die to your old man and all of the foolish works of the flesh.

Wisdom is the most powerful force in the universe.

The wisdom of God is more powerful than all of the wisdom of this world and the wisdom of the devil.

Your whole life will change once you start walking in God's wisdom.

One of the wisest things you can do is study God's Word to obey every truth you find in it.

You will be proved to be a wise person if the Holy Spirit always leads you.

You have to eradicate the image of a fool out of your heart if you are going to walk in the wisdom of God.

Doing anything clearly violating God's Word is one of the most foolish things you can do in this life.

The smartest thing you can do in this life is walk in the wisdom of God.

Being led by the Holy Spirit of God is one of the wisest things you can ever do in this life.

One of the fastest ways to get God on your side is to listen to all of His wisdom.

If you want to be honored by God, then listen to all of His eternal Divine wisdom.

Walking in the wisdom of God will lead you to great honor, and respect and give you an eternal legacy.

The wisdom of God has the power to make you a legend.

There are no riches on this earth or in the entire universe comparable to the eternal wisdom of God.

The wisdom of God will take you to places you never dreamed were possible.

The wisdom of God has an inexpressible beauty to those who are privileged enough to see and possess her.

Those who value and hold in high regard the wisdom of God feast on her words daily.

It is a luxury to have the inside of your soul filled with the wisdom of God.

Wisdom tastes better than any known food to man, and if you are wise, you will indulge yourself at her table.

Waking up to the wisdom of God talking to you every morning is one of the most valuable and precious moments you can ever experience in this life.

Nothing is comparable to the wisdom of God.

Listening to the wisdom of God daily is more entertaining than all of the movies and pleasures of this life put together.

Foolish people have no idea what they are missing out on when it comes to the wisdom of God.

If you want the wisdom of God to dwell in your heart, you will have to commit to listening to and adhering to all of her advice.

You have to allow God to change your image into a wise son of God if you are going to be able to fit into the garment of His Divine wisdom.

❝I didn't know exactly what I was missing out on until wisdom entered into my heart and I started treasuring her for the prize she is.

It's not wise to come against a wise man of God.

It takes wisdom from God to work miracles.

There is a great responsibility that comes with walking in the wisdom of God and being a wise person.

Any advice that is contrary to the wisdom of God is not wisdom.

Any knowledge that does not align with God's doctrines is not wise to listen to.

Just because you have the knowledge of God doesn't mean you are wise.

Just because you are knowledgeable doesn't mean you are wise.

I love the wisdom of God more than life itself because there is no life without true wisdom from God.

What could God do with a man or woman of God who completely gave over their entire life to embrace all of the Divine wisdom of God?

When the spirit of wisdom lifts off someone, they immediately go back to being a fool.

If someone is truly filled with the Holy Spirit they will also be filled with the wisdom of God.

A mark of being filled with the Holy Spirit is having God's wisdom resting upon you.

If you desire to be wise, you must allow God to burn out all foolishness in your heart.

God doesn't just want to give you wisdom; He wants to make you a wise person.

Embracing the wisdom of God is the wisest thing you can do in this life.

A wise man confronts the evil in their own heart first before he confronts the evil in others.

To be a wise person, you must commit to letting the voice of wisdom speak in every area of your life.

Wise people understand that not everyone is going to listen to what they have to say.

Wise people only reveal God's deep hidden wise counsel to those who are ready to heed their advice.

God has a large stockpile of wisdom that He is willing to freely give to the person who will listen and take heed to what He has to say.

Don't just seek for wisdom, but seek to be a wise person because it's easy for a wise person to find wisdom.

Building, creating, and inventing things correctly takes a lot of wisdom.

You have to let wisdom intertwine with your conscience if you seek to be a wise person.

You have to make a full unwavering commitment to the wisdom of God in all areas of your life to be a wise person.

Jesus Christ is the embodiment of all wisdom.

Wisdom will make you prosperous.

Wise people listen to the wisdom of the Holy Spirit all of the time.

The only way to become wise is to listen to the Holy Spirit as He teaches you out of the Word of God.

Wise people know how to quickly handle and deal with every situation that comes before them.

Wise people make wise decisions and always learn from any mistake.

A wise person weighs out their actions before they make a move.

❝ The wisdom of God will pull your thoughts and focus from the natural temporal world and into the eternal purposes of God.

Walking in wisdom drives away fear and paranoia.

It is unwise to doubt God and live in fear.

There is a wise answer from God for every problem a person faces.

A wise person thinks and talks about wisdom all of the time.

Wisdom first starts with a choice to listen to the instruction and correction of God, and then it manifests in you becoming a wise person.

The wise rest safe and secure daily in the arms of wisdom.

A wise person is not afraid to look over all of their thoughts, words, and actions and judge themselves.

A wise person evaluates themselves and ensures they adhere to the Word of God in all areas of their life.

You can tell how wise a man is by the type of woman he is attracted to and marries.

One of the highest honors you could receive in this life is for God to say you are a wise person.

It's wise to be led by the Spirit at all times.

If you don't embrace all of the wisdom of God, you will not be mature enough to handle a real anointing from God.

The wisdom of God is the Anointing of God.

You can find a lot of wisdom in your darkest hours.

If someone is not anointed, it's because they are not wise.

Wisdom is one of the most powerful forces in the universe.

James 1:5-7 (KJV)
5 If any of you lack wisdom, let him ask of God, that giveth to all men liberally, and upbraideth not; and it shall be given him. 6 But let him ask in faith, nothing wavering. For he that wavereth is like a wave of the sea driven with the wind and tossed. 7 For let not that man think that he shall receive any thing of the Lord.

CHAPTER 42

※

Word of God

❝God can be found in His Word, and when you get the Word of God in you, God will be found in you.

You have to believe the Word of God coming out of your mouth more than what is going on around you for you to inherit the promises of God.

You can't walk in a spiritual truth from God's Word if your eyes are not opened to it, but the more your spiritual eyes are opened to the mystery of God's Kingdom, the more you can walk in it!

When people don't do what God's Word says and fail, they still blame God or someone else for their failure.

When you're looking to obey things in the Bible, make sure you obey Christ's tough Words and sayings.

Just because someone reads their Bible doesn't mean they are listening to the voice of the Holy Spirit.

The more I read the Bible, the more I clearly see that God wants to work miracles.

I don't want just to know the Word; I want to know the God of the Word.

Sometimes, I wonder if people are reading the same Bible as I am.

God has given us a blueprint in His Word on how to win the war of words.

You must ask Divine questions to get to Divine truths in the Word of God.

The Word of God forms belief systems, but not everyone ends up with the same belief system who reads the Word of God. This is why we need men of God that are sent by God to help us understand the Word of God.

To know God, you have to spend time in the Word of God so you can hear the voice of God speak to you through the Scriptures.

Faith has no problem waiting as long as it takes for God to fulfill His Word.

If you only speak and live the Word of God, you will never be judged because God doesn't judge Himself.

A true man of God teaches you things out of the Word of God that you've never seen before.

You have to become the Words of Christ.

Knowledge of the Scriptures without making decisions on that knowledge is useless.

The Word of God reveals who God is.

The Word of God was written to teach us what to believe because what you believe is what you speak, and what you speak is what manifests in your life.

You have to stay in the timing of God's Word to receive His blessings.

The law of God reveals the glory and image of God.

The glory of God is revealed in the Word of God.

The Word of God is the image of God revealed.

❝❝ All failure comes from a lack of understanding God's Word.

One thought from God's Word can change your life forever.

If the Word of God is not challenging you, you are not hearing the Word of God.

You have to read the Bible through the eyes of faith, or you will end up with wrong interpretations.

Adhering to, keeping, and obeying the Words of Christ will make you great and carry you into eternity.

I don't just want to know the Scriptures; I want to know the Holy Spirit who inspired the Scriptures.

There is a place where you can get to in your obedience to the Word of God that nothing can shake you.

The closer you get to God, the slower and deeper you read the Bible.

You have to keep all the Words of Christ to experience the Father.

Nothing excites me more than studying God's Word and being in His presence.

Nothing can replace the Word of God in your life.

The Word of God speaks to the heart, cleanses the soul, and transforms the mind.

Changing your thoughts to line up with the thoughts from God's Word is what changes you, not just reading your Bible.

No book or sermon can replace reading and studying God's Word for yourself.

It's not just reading the Word of God that changes you; what changes you is when you understand and obey what you read in the Word of God.

Obeying all the Words of Christ is the only way to prove your love for the Father.

If you truly want to be made free, you need to eat up the Word of God.

It's important to keep your mind on the Word of God because of all the evil forces and voices in this world that try to distract and pull you off course from doing God's will.

No weapon, enemy, or foe can withstand a strike from the sword of God's Word delivered by a man or woman of God.

Whoever does the will of God and obeys His Word is my true family.

You have to spend a lot of time meditating on God's Word and thoughts to grow up and mature in Christ.

Some people are bothered by what the Bible says. I am bothered by people who are bothered by the Word of God.

It amazes me how people can read the same Bible and walk away with two or more totally different interpretations.

It takes years to refine and polish the Word of God inside of you.

You have to live the Word of God boldly.

66 **There's a lot of preaching these days that is just self-help and motivational speaking, not the Word of God.**

You will find God when you meditate on the Word of God.

God is looking to bless anyone who hears, understands, meditates on, and does the Word of God.

You cannot base your belief system based upon your experiences or the experiences of others. It must be based completely upon the Word of God.

It's not how much you read or know of the Bible that matters, but how much you conformed to the teachings of the Bible in your life that matters.

Hebrews 4:12 (KJV)

For the word of God is quick, and powerful, and sharper than any twoedged sword, piercing even to the dividing asunder of soul and spirit, and of the joints and marrow, and is a discerner of the thoughts and intents of the heart.

CHAPTER 43

⬥

Words

❝You can be defeated or win a great victory based on what you say or don't say.

Change your words, and you will change your life.

If you don't like your life, change what you are saying about your life. Say what you want your life to be, not what it presently is.

All victory is just a few thoughts and words away.

You have to learn to live out of the image created by the words spoken to you by the Holy Spirit.

Words control and dictate your whole life.

The only way you will defeat the devil is by God weaponizing your words by His Spirit.

Understanding the power of your words and how they can affect the outcome and destiny of your life is a truth that cannot be underestimated.

When someone comes to a mature understanding of the power of their words, they are no longer a victim of circumstances but a ruler of their destiny.

God grants us to have whatever we are speaking.

Proverbs 18:21 (KJV)
Death and life are in the power of the tongue: and they that love it shall eat the fruit thereof.

CHAPTER 44

❦

Worry

❝ 99% of things people worry about never happen, and even if they did happen, God has the power to fix it.

All stress starts and continues with someone not living in God's will.

When you are right with God, you don't have to worry about anything.

The problem with worry is it empowers the problem you are thinking about.

One of the biggest curses to hit humankind after the fall of Adam is the curse of worrying.

When you are seeking first the kingdom of God and His righteousness, there is nothing to worry about.

Worrying is mentally tormenting for those who engage in it.

Just because bad news comes or circumstances occur contrary to God's Word, it doesn't have to trigger worry.

If you are living right and full of faith, worry is no longer a triggered response to negative news.

Worry and stress are only triggered by those not seeking the kingdom of God and His righteousness first.

To get to a place where you are worry-free in this life, you will have to commit yourself totally to God and His Kingdom and spend a lot of time in prayer and studying God's Word.

When an evil report comes, don't allow your mind to go down the road of fear, doubt, and worry.

Bad news comes to everyone at some point in this life, and when it does, Christians have a God who is present and eagerly there to help and deliver them.

Worry is a mental choice people make, and so is faith in God. What choice will you make when you find yourself in a situation that contradicts what God's Word says?

Worry is a big part of the curse that came on mankind after the fall, and they did have things that could harm them because they were outside of the protection of God.

Your job is to stay and dwell in the secret place under the shadow of the Almighty, God's job is to protect and deliver you.

If you are not living right before God, you do have a lot to be worried and stressed out about.

It's not our job to worry about how or if God is going to answer your prayers and meet your needs. It's God's job to **answer prayers anyway He wants to and anytime He wants to. Let God be God.**

I refuse to allow my mind to worry about things after all that God has shown me.

Worry about nothing, and believe God for everything.

You need to ask God to forgive you for worrying about things He has already taken care of before you got there.

❝Worry is an unfair response to God who has shown Himself over and over again that He has everything under control.

The devil loves to mentally torture people through worry and fear.

I used to think worrying was something I was obligated to do when I was faced with problems, but it's not.

Christians who worry are disrespecting their All Powerful God.

You no longer have to put up with thoughts of worry.

Philippians 4:6-7 (KJV)
6 Be careful for nothing; but in every thing by prayer and supplication with thanksgiving let your requests be made known unto God. 7 And the peace of God, which passeth all understanding, shall keep your hearts and minds through Christ Jesus.

CHAPTER 45

⚜

Miscellaneous

❝❝Don't give away what you have in God so easily.

I refuse to be domesticated by the world or religious system.

You can't live in the old man and expect new man results.

Those who don't cry out to God during the storm will be the one's still crying after the storm.

When evil and aggressive, oppressive governments arise, God will raise up even more powerful men and women of God to defeat them.

When we see problems, God sees answers.

God has an answer for any problem the devil can try to throw at you.

You can never injure a true man of God, even if you kill him.

God will only send you when you have been prepared and are ready to be sent.

You have to focus on God until you can see Him clearly.

It amazes me how people cannot see God when He is all around them.

God has been working on your behalf even before you were born.

I listen to the voice of God for correction and not to the voice of abusive religious people.

Christians must be more dangerous than the dangers that face them.

True Christians are tough as nails.

You cannot do what a superhero does unless you are a superhero.

Be ready for anything, get offended at nothing, love everyone, forgive everything, and God can use you anywhere.

I will not change who I am in God or leave the Secret Place, no matter what is going on around me.

When God is taking His time, He is planning something awesome for you.

When God makes a promise, He will go to great lengths to fulfill it.

A Christian can't have a demon, that's why when I cast it out it has to go.

In the Old Testament, messing with a man of God was never a good idea.

Appreciation goes a long way with God and, for that matter, with everyone else.

Start every day by declaring what you want out of life, and you will get it.

Make sure you keep ascending like an eagle until you break out above the fog and clouds.

Don't you dare try to muzzle my mouth when I am speaking for God.

Everything you do always affects someone else, either in a good or bad way.

God wants you to love Him back as much as He loves you.

Be careful what you look at because it will cause your heart to focus on it.

❝❝ *God is with you as much as you are with Him.*

The more you are with God, the more He is with you.

If you want God to be with you, make sure you are with Him in all your ways.

There is no room in the Holy of Holies for a bitter person.

Integrity is doing what's right when no one is looking and when everyone is looking.

If you have something and don't know you have it, it is as good as not having it.

If you have something and don't know how to use it, it is as good as not having it.

When you miss the timing of the Lord, you will think you are cursed when you are just out of sync.

A big part of being blessed includes knowing what to do and when to do it.

Apologies don't mean anything if you keep doing what you are saying you are sorry for.

Faithfulness to God unlocks God's calling on your life, both now and in the coming age.

God is looking for faithful believers He can trust.

The only thing connecting you to this created world is your flesh and blood.

When you are right with God, you ALWAYS win.

Some people don't think the Lord cares about their attitude, but He does.

One man with God is always the majority.

Restoration of the soul is a process.

When you have the favor of God in your life, people start promoting and treating you better because they see the blessing of God on you.

God has more control over the factors that govern your life than you may ever fully realize.

You have very little control over most things in your life and you must deeply trust in God for everything.

Spiritual growth takes daily dying to yourself.

The Kingdom is entered into by those who daily grow up spiritually in God.

Never resist change because change is a big part of life.

You have to go through the desert to get to the Promised Land.

Thankfulness and a good attitude go a long way with the Lord.

Many men of God in the Bible were called despite their past.

Your past does not define your future.

It's a wonderful day when you wake up, see, and walk in the full plan of God for your life.

My tolerance for evil is at an all-time low.

My tolerance for the spirit of Jezebel is at an all-time low.

Life is BORING without God.

❝What good is living if you can't have daily interaction with God?

The judgment brings the blessing.

We need the influence of God Almighty in every part of our life.

You prove you are with the Lord by what you do and what you don't do.

God mirrors people.

The conversation of the Godhead is not for everyone.

Your body has to change and become adaptable to the speech of God.

You could know all about the rapture and still miss it if you don't live ready as Jesus taught.

You can get to a place in your walk with God where you can see Him who is invisible.

You have to learn to live in a place where God can use you.

Grow up and act like Christ.

You cannot underestimate the role that frankincense, myrrh, and spikenard played in the life of Jesus.

The moment you wake up and realize you don't have what it takes is the day you can begin to find in God what it takes.

In light of all God has done for us, how can you not love Him and serve Him with all your might?

Your bed is meant to be a holy place where God can commune with you at night, so you better keep it holy.

Just because they are family doesn't mean they have your best interests in mind.

With God, nothing is ever over until He says it's over. Even death cannot stop or get in the way of God.

There is no one, and I mean absolutely no one, who has more pure motives towards you than God Almighty.

Never believe a lie that God is not good in any way, shape, or form. Just because you may not understand something doesn't mean God isn't good. You just don't have all of the facts.

So many people have married outside of the will of God only to be distracted and miss out on the call of God on their life.

God always has the last say on everything that happens inside His created universe.

There is a generation who will forsake everything to take up the call of God.

When the Lord is chastening you, the best thing to do is to run to Him, not from Him.

You can find great power while waiting on God.

When someone talks and makes no sense, they have the curse of Babel on them.

Immature, negative, evil, confusing, and vain speaking comes from the curse of Babel being on someone.

The biggest healing that can happen to a Christian is a timely death.

❝ When you have a real walk with God in private, you don't' have to fake that you have something with God in public.

When you love God with all of your heart, soul, mind, body, and strength, He will spoil you.

I am neither for you nor against you; I am on the Lord's side. Whose side are you on?

I don't have time for your nonsense; get right with God or get out of my way.

Random acts of kindness should be a big part of a Christian's life.

Sometimes, silence or a whisper is the only appropriate thing to do when you are in the presence of God Almighty.

I hate injustice at every level.

We have to take on and defeat injustice at every level in society.

Your bed is a Holy, special place between you and God that must always be protected from defilement.

If you want to be an overcomer in this life, you are going to have to get violent about the things of God.

You have a lot to learn if you don't think the Lord never gets angry.

In the long run, the only person who can cause you to be cursed is yourself.

You are kidding yourself and don't know the Bible very well if you don't think God has a selection and weeding-out process.

People have to earn the privilege to speak into your life.

An abundance of money only expands the horizons of the wicked.

Don't make me regret letting you into my life.

Seasons and the feasts of the Lord are very important with the timing of the Lord.

Everything I preach about I wasn't. I received all of this from God.

You should try to bless everyone who comes across your path in some way.

Some people are looking and scrambling to find another reason or person to blame for their faults, cursing their life.

It is your responsibility to hear from God for yourself.

If you want to be right with God, always do what is right before the Lord.

Some of the greatest things God does have never been seen by anyone for years.

Only go where God sends you and at the time when He wants you to go.

Just because someone calls themselves a Christian doesn't mean they are speaking for God.

The moment you start making excuses for your failures is when you start puking on yourself for all to see.

People who live in a spirit of anger are like raging bulls that chase down and attack anything in front of them, good and bad.

Uncontrolled anger is like a raging bull that sees red and runs it down just because he's mad at the world.

There is no nobility in the rage of a bull.

I have to continually keep my finger upon the pulse of my mind, as well as my will and emotions, to keep them constantly focused on God and His Kingdom.

❝ My relationship with God is the number one thing I am working on.

How dare you try to speak over my life and say something God hasn't said.

Giving to others activates giving to you.

When you have God, you have everything at your disposal.

In Christianity, if you are not going forward, you are going backward because there is no standing still.

Your personal experience should never dictate your belief system from the Bible.

You can't disobey God's laws and think everything's going to be okay.

Giving activates giving.

Real champions are very humble.

Someone is going to get blessed tonight.

You can't afford not to give.

All the answers you seek in this life are found in the Bible; you just have to dig deep to get to them.

A man without God is very limited.

You should spend most of your day doing things of eternal value.

God uses the poor for the righteous to show their love for Christ when you give to them.

A greedy person hates to give.

The secrets of God are not for everyone.

Everything is going to be okay if God is with you.

I don't care what you have done in the past; I want to know what you are doing right now for God.

To break lust off of your life, you have to train yourself to quit looking at women.

I refuse to let God down during this great time in history.

God is looking for men and women that He can make legends out of.

A betrayer usually ends up committing suicide to deal with their demons.

A betrayer has to kill himself because he can't live with himself.

What good is a pile of money if you are sick and dying?

Far too many Christians have been domesticated by the world and religion.

Don't ever try to domesticate a man of God.

A true man or woman of God is wild and dangerous by nature.

If you act and talk like a victim, you will become a victim.

Supernatural demonic problems need Supernatural Divine answers.

❝ The Kingdom of God has never been and will never be in a recession.

Extraordinary times call for extraordinary people.

Tough times call for tougher people.

Dangerous times call for dangerous men and women of God.

Current events will create opportunities for unknown heroes to arise out of nowhere and be used by God to save the day.

Anything and everything has to be approved by God in this universe.

The good and the evil are all subject to the authority and power of God Almighty.

There is no better discipline than self-discipline.

You are fooling yourself if you don't realize that God is the BOSS running the whole show.

The speed at which you act upon a new truth will determine your success.

Some of God's greatest works are done secretly in the hearts of men, and it takes years before they are manifested.

I am ready to accept any and all consequences for believing in and serving the Lord Jesus Christ.

There is a Spirit behind every characteristic of God, and these are some of God's greatest treasures.

I live where the eagles fly.

I would rather have lots of God and His Kingdom than lots of money.

There are two kingdoms: the Kingdom of God and the kingdom of darkness. People want God to come into their kingdom of darkness and fix problems, but the problem is only fixed by them coming into the Kingdom of God.

God has to create the man to do the ministry He wants to be accomplished on the earth.

When I have to go to God and start talking about someone's bad behavior, it is not a good thing for them if they don't repent.

The more you are with God, the more He is with you.

To be someone great is a daily choice.

Serving God comes down to choices.

Your experiences will match your beliefs.

Adam ate of the tree in rebellion, but Jesus died on the tree in obedience.

Always take care of the birds wherever you live because God would do that.

People want to know about the father of great sons because they can see their fathering skills in the sons they produce.

If you are 100% with God, God will be with you 100%.

If a son is great, they must have a great father who knows how to train up his children in the ways of the Lord.

Don't wait for people to tell you who you are; show them who God said you are until they believe it.

You have to treat all of the Commands of God with proper respect because disobeying God's Commands disrespects God, because He established all Laws from who He is and all that He stands for.

66 You will not be shaken when God builds a rock-solid image of Christ within you.

It is easy to change what you do if you first change who you are first.

When you obey God and are led by His Spirit, you can always look into your future and know that God will be there to take care of you.

Don't try to do something great, be something great, and you will do great things.

Part of the curse of God is for Him to just ignore you.

Whatever you watch, read, and listen to is what you are filling your soul with and telling your affections to love.

True prophetic insight will only come to those who walk in the mature wisdom of God.

You can learn a lot about a man by the type of woman he is attracted to.

Who you become is more important than what you do in this life.

Just because God loves you doesn't mean He is with you. You also have to be with Him for that.

Always choose the Creator over His creation.

There comes a point in everyone's life when they will be faced with the decision of choosing between the Creator or His creation.

Once you choose the Creator over all of creation then all of creation will start working for you.

The curse of Solomon is that in all his wisdom, he didn't choose the Creator over the creation.

How can you know if something does or doesn't work if you haven't tried it?

A distracted mind is a defeated mind.

You can learn a lot about someone by how they treat animals.

Be careful not to love something that is killing you or could kill you.

God can be trusted more than anyone in this universe.

Never fear what God might ask you to do because He will be with you if you obey Him.

When the devil comes with problems, God comes with answers.

There is always an answer to a problem; you just have to find it.

In your darkest hour, if you seek God, He will be a light unto you.

The greater the darkness, the greater the light.

God doesn't want to be surrounded by people throughout all of eternity who were only motivated by what He could do for them.

You have to ask yourself if your only motive for serving God is because of what He has done or can do for you.

Some of the best messages ever preached pissed most of the listeners off.

Beware of spiritual laziness because it will cause you to want to sleep when you should be praying or reading your Bible.

Spiritual laziness will rob you of spiritual strength.

Spiritual laziness will always hit you right before a big event in God and cause you not to be ready.

A Jezebelic spirit speaks from a prophetic devil of lust that wants to prophesy your death.

66 *A distracted Christian is a defeated Christian.*

Growing up in God is not easy.

Take your calling seriously because the stakes are high.

The stakes couldn't be higher regarding your walk with God.

You're calling from God; it is not a job; it's a relationship.

You never want God to stop being jealous of you.

Never let a person take a place in your heart where only God belongs.

Wrong women can bring in unnecessary demonic attacks on your life.

The devil likes to use women to destroy men's lives.

Sometimes, the prettier a woman is, the more demons she has.

The things you go through, you grow through.

Make sure you live rapture-ready.

The rebuke of God fixes things.

God will rebuke you for not rebuking things.

I would rather live in an apartment with God than in a mansion with the devil.

You cannot run from the judgments of God forever.

People who know how to speak to mountains and make them move change the world.

There are no shortcuts to greatness.

Time flies when you are in anointing.

Believing God is personal, and He honors those who honor and believe in Him.

God is looking for someone He can send out that people can model their life after.

With God, it's never over.

When you are under the complete authority of Jesus as your Lord, you have the right to call upon His Name for deliverance.

Don't waste your death without dying a death that glorifies God.

One day, the Lord will tell you to be perfect as you get closer to Him.

God is in absolute control of EVERYTHING!

Someone has to pay a price for the yoke to be broken.

You have to go through the death, burial, and resurrection in your own life to defeat the devil.

You can't try to minister in the power of God without understanding the death, burial, and resurrection of Jesus Christ.

The answer to all of life's problems is the preaching of the Gospel.

The Holy Spirit cannot help anyone outside of the Gospel.

The Holy Ghost will come upon you with power when you're ready to be a witness of the resurrection of the Lord Jesus Christ.

❝ The primary purpose of the Holy Spirit on the earth is to help people receive all that Jesus accomplished through His death, burial, and resurrection.

The power of the Holy Spirit enforces all of the blessings Jesus paid for us through His death, burial, and resurrection.

Talking to and hanging out with the wrong people can mess your spirit up.

We minister out of who we become and not just what we know.

You have not because you ask, believe, and declare not.

If you listen to God, God will listen to you.

Your name represents all that something was created to be.

The Holy Spirit is the hand of the Lord that obeys the voice of God.

You have to protect the blessing of God in your life.

If you are not a Christian, you are The Walking Dead.

I am an overcoming, victorious, conquering warrior because God is with me.

There is no sound on the earth like the blowing of the shofar.

You can't act like Esau and have Isaac bless you with the blessing of Abraham.

I am outcome-independent.

If you don't have a secret walk with God, then you probably have a secret walk with the devil.

An overcomer overcame something, a conquer conquered something and a winner won something. What have you overcome, conquered, or won?

An overcomer needs something to overcome, a conquer needs something to conquer, and a winner needs something to win.

Being an overcomer is not an option if you want to go to Heaven.

You must see yourself as something great before you can do something great.

Humility plays a big part in you becoming made in the image of Christ.

You have to see yourself the way God sees you before you can defeat the devil or any of your enemies.

No one can steal your wealth or currency in God.

You are as good as dead if you don't have God.

The deeper you get with God, the lonelier you'll be.

In God's eyes, death is anything not functioning according to His intended will or purpose.

Whenever the Holy Spirit falls, it is a critical moment in history.

Swing for the fences, and you will knock it out of the park.

It's a critical moment in your life's history when God comes near you.

The fear of God is a weapon.

❝ *Every warrior needs a giant to defeat.*

It takes determination when speaking to a mountain to make it move.

If you are not a servant to God, how can you expect things to serve you?

Sometimes, the very ones you were sent to minister to are the ones who end up betraying you.

All defeat comes by not knowing who you are in God.

Anything that is not operating under the commands and will and Word of God is considered dead in God's eyes.

Anything that is sick, diseased, deformed, and not working according to its intended purpose is considered dead in God's eyes.

You can never kill a true Christian.

The whole law of Moses was mainly written for Jesus, and when He came and fulfilled it, it was done away with.

All things have to be spoken into existence; they don't just come to pass.

Abstinence is more fulfilling than going after the lust of the flash.

There were only two reasons for someone not to be healed. The lack of someone being anointed. Or the lack of someone not believing in that anointing.

God gave the law through Moses to prepare people for the Messiah and for the Messiah to fulfill the law, and once it was fulfilled, He did away with it and established a new law.

If you don't start asking Divine questions, you cannot dig into the deep things of God.

God will do whatever you can believe Him for.

Everyone is put in the garden of their own life and has to tend to it in the things of God.

You cannot teach without fully knowing a subject, and you cannot fully know a subject without deep meditation and study.

Life would be scary to live without God, but I am not without God; therefore, life is not scary.

Divine questions receive Divine answers.

The more they fight you, the more God will vindicate you.

The more you are attacked, the more God will go out of His way to defend you.

When you start sounding more like Jesus, you will be attacked and persecuted.

You cannot separate the messenger from the message.

Anything that turns your heart away from God is idolatry.

Romans 15:29 (KJV)
And I am sure that, when I come unto you, I shall come in the fulness of the blessing of the gospel of Christ.

Smith

Wigglesworth

Quotes

CHAPTER 46

Devotion

❝Looking at me with tears in his eyes, he said, when are you going to move into a realm that you have not yet touched and get going for God?

David du Plessis asked Smith Wigglesworth a week before he died: Mr. Wigglesworth, who are you going to give your mantle to when you die? He replied, I am not done with it myself yet. A week later he was in a church in Wakefield to speak at a friend's funeral. He was in the vestry, seeking the presence of God, when they heard him take his last breath. They ran into the vestry, but he was gone. He had not given his mantle to anybody.

It is better to live ready than to get ready!

Every new revelation brings a new dedication. Let us seek Him.

If you are living in the earth realm and expect things from Heaven, they will never come.

We are dull of comprehension because we so often let the cares of this world blind our eyes; but if we can be open to God, we shall see that He has a greater plan for us in the future than we have ever seen in the past.

If you have lost your hunger for God, if you do not have a cry for more of God, you are missing the plan. There must come up from us a cry that cannot be satisfied with anything but God.

Far too many people spend their entire lifetime making a living. Making a living is the small, timeserving, dwarfed and paralyzed man's object. Making a life is the kingly, righteous and holy man's object. The one lives in the narrow, prison-limited circle of self, and the other in a world which is bound only when infinity and eternity have limits.

Give attention to life's inflow; outward service will dwindle if inward energies are not renewed.

Never look back if you want the power of God in your life. You will find out that in the measure you have allowed yourself to look back, you have missed what God had for you.

You must come to the place of daily building with a daily denial of self, a daily discipline of reading and meditating on the Word of God, a daily habit of spending quality time in worship and waiting on Him, and a daily seeking Him for more.

It is God's delight to make possible to us that which seems impossible, and when we reach a place where He alone has right of way, then all the things that have been misty and misunderstood are cleared up.

The secret of spiritual success is a hunger that persists. It is an awful condition to be satisfied with one's spiritual attainments. God was and is looking for hungry, thirsty people.

You can lose more in ten minutes than you have gained in a whole year in the Assembly.

God brings us to a place where the difficulties are, where the pressure is, where the hard corner is, where everything is so difficult that you know that there are no possibilities on the human side. God must do it.

I am always on my merit. Every time I preach, I preach my best. Every time I pray, I pray my best.

Transformation comes through constantly yielding. This is the only way. You can go to Church all your life; you can spend all your time learning, praying and singing; but still, you will be captive to your past unless you make the decision to yield and obey every time God shows you something.

We must be emptied of self and filled with God.

66 **Far too many of us dwell on the lowlands of salvation. Can't you hear voices calling you to the uplands of Divine grace? Mountain climbing is thrilling! Let's be off! Hebron's heights rise before us. Shall we explore our unclaimed inheritance in the Heavenlies?**

People could be built far greater in the Lord and be more wonderfully established if they would move out sometimes and think over the graces of the Lord.

The devil knows if he can capture your thought life he has won a mighty victory over you.

God never intended His people to be ordinary or commonplace. His intentions were that they should be on fire for Him, conscious of His Divine power, realizing the glory of the cross that foreshadows the crown.

Before a man can bind the enemy, he must know there is nothing binding him.

In me is working a power stronger than any other power.

Before God could bring me to this place He has broken me a thousand times.

The power of God will take you out of your own plans and put you into the plan of God.

Beloved, let me entreat you to pay any price. Never mind what it costs; it is worth all to have His smile, to have His presence.

God has privileged us in Christ Jesus to live above the ordinary human plane of life. Those who want to be ordinary and live on a lower plane can do so, but as for me, I will not.

I have wept, I have groaned, I have travailed many a night until God broke me. It seems to me that until God has mowed you down you never can have this longsuffering for others.

Will you let Him have your will; will you let Him, have you? If you will, all His power is at your disposal.

A man is in a great place when he has no one to turn to but God.

To live two days in succession on the same spiritual plane is a tragedy.

The Lord would so cleanse the motive and desires of our hearts that we will seek but one thing only, and that is, His glory.

You can have a good reputation in your Church, you can say all the right words, you can even know all the right phrases and all the right answers, and still be powerless. Powerlessness is the result of not having the resemblance of Jesus in your spirit. The resemblance of Jesus Christ's likeness comes through a surrendered life.

We can only receive power as a gift, through yielding and obeying.

The man that stops gets nothing. Oh, don't stop at Jericho; don't stop at Jordan; don't stop anywhere when God would have you move on into all of His fullness that He has for you.

It is God's delight to make possible to us that which seems impossible, and when we reach a place where He alone has right of way, then all the things that have been misty and misunderstood are cleared up.

The life that is in me is a thousand times bigger than I am outside.

No matter what troubles you, God can shake the devil out, and completely transform you. There is none like Him.

Are you ready? What for? Ready to believe God! Ready to catch the vision of what God has for you! Ready to enter right into God's plan for you today!

❝ *I don't ask myself how I feel, I tell myself how I feel.*

Increase comes by action, by using what we have and what we know.

It pays to trust God with all and to make no reservation.

If you examine yourself, you will be natural, but if you look at God, you will be supernatural.

I refuse to be an ordinary man. You say, why do you? Because I have an extraordinary God who makes extraordinary people.

I am satisfied with the dissatisfaction that never rests until it is satisfied and satisfied again.

God's will shall be done, provided your will is not in the way.

You have Divine personality, but you will know the mightiness of its workings only as you venture. You cannot be with me at anytime, anywhere, but I am after God.

The most trying time is the most helpful time. Beloved, if you read the Scriptures, you will never find anything about an easy time, and if you are really reconstructed it will be in a hard time. It will not be in a singing meeting, but at a time when you think all things are dried up and that there is no hope for you. Then is the time that God makes the man or woman.

You must every day make higher ground. You must deny yourself to get on with God. You must refuse everything that is not pure and holy and separate. God wants you pure in heart. He wants your intense desire to be after holiness.

If you are in the same place as you were yesterday, you are a backslider.

Philippians 3:7-8 (KJV)
7 But what things were gain to me, those I counted loss for Christ. 8 Yea doubtless, and I count all things but loss for the excellency of the knowledge of Christ Jesus my Lord: for whom I have suffered the loss of all things, and do count them but dung, that I may win Christ,

CHAPTER 47

Faith

❝ I am not moved by what I see or feel but by what I believe.

God would pass over a million people just to find someone who believes Him.

Unbelief can be very blind, but faith can see through a stone wall.

Inactivity of faith is a robber, which steals blessing.

Great faith is the product of great fights.

Fear looks, Faith jumps.

Great testimonies are the outcome of great tests. Great triumphs can only come out of great trials.

All lack of faith is due to not feeding on God's Word.

I believe that there is only one way to all the treasures of God, and that is the way of faith.

The only reason for healing not to occur was a lack of faith.

The end of all real faith always is rejoicing.

There is no limit to what our limitless God will do in response to a limitless faith.

There is nothing impossible with God. All the impossibility is with us when we measure God by the limitations of our unbelief.

Faith never fails to obtain its objective.

I believe God will always turn out to meet you on a special line if you dare to believe Him.

Ask for what you want; believe, receive from God, and thank God for it.

It is one thing to say you have faith, and another thing to be in a tight corner and prove it.

God wants us all to have an audacity of faith that dares to believe for all that is set forth in the Word.

There are two kinds of faith. There is the natural faith. But the supernatural faith is the gift of God.

Without faith, you have nothing. You cannot be saved without it. You cannot be healed without it.

Nothing in the world glorifies God so much as simple rest of faith in what God's Word says.

Faith is an act.

When faith lays hold, impossibilities must yield.

The faith of Christ never wavers. When you have that faith, the thing, what you need is finished.

A prayer without faith is without accomplishment.

I long to be in a great revival that will eclipse anything we have ever thought of. I have faith to believe it is coming.

Being hard-hearted, critical or unforgiving will hinder faith quicker than anything.

66 God wants to give you a faith that shakes hell!

To the man of Faith there is not a thing that is not opportunity.

Faith has a deaf ear to the devil and to the working of the natural mind, and a big ear to God. Faith has a deaf ear to yourself, and an open ear to God. Faith won't take any notice of feelings. Faith says you are complete in Him.

May God help you to never stop persevering till you get what you want. Let your aspiration be large and your faith rise until you are wholly on fire for God's best.

It is like receiving a gift; you don't know that you have it till you act in faith.

Faith is better than feelings, and if you have faith, you will have all the feelings you can feel.

Your life must be one of going from Faith to Faith.

Thousands have missed wonderful blessings because they have not had faith to move out and begin in the natural, in faith that the Lord would take them into the realm of the supernatural.

How can one come to possess great faith? Now listen, here is the answer to that: First, the blade, then the ear, then the full corn in the ear. Faith must grow by soil, moisture, and exercise.

The power of God is just the same today as it was in the past. Men need to be taken back to the old paths, to the old-time faith, to believing God's Word and every 'Thus says the Lord' in it.

Desire toward God and you will have desires from God and He will meet you on the line of those desires when you reach out in simple faith.

And as I saw, in the presence of God, the limitations of my faith, there came another faith, a faith that could not be denied, a faith that took the promise, a faith that believed God's Word. And from that presence, I came back again to earth, but not the same man. God gave a faith that could shake hell and anything else.

Believe that when you come into the presence of God you can have all you came for. You can take it away, and you can use it, for all the power of God is at your disposal in response to your faith.

Faith is the audacity that rejoices in the fact that God cannot break His own Word. Faith is not agitation. It is quiet confidence that God means what He says, and we act on His Word.

Faith is just the open door through which the Lord comes. Do not say 'I was saved by faith' or 'I was healed by faith'. Faith does not save and heal. God saves and heals through that open door.

As this like precious faith becomes a part of you, it will make you so that you will dare to do anything. And remember, God wants daring men, men who will dare all, men who will be strong in Him and dare to do exploits. How shall we reach this plane of faith? Let go your own thoughts, and take the thoughts of God, the Word of God.

Two things will get you to leap out of yourselves into the promises of God today. One is purity, and the other is FAITH, which is kindled more and more BY PURITY.

No wavering. This is the principle: He who believes is definite. A definite faith brings a definite experience and a definite utterance.

Now, who wants to get nearer to God? Who would like a special blessing? Let everybody who is hungry for God stand on his feet. Everybody who is in real earnest move forward. If you move forward only a foot, it will show that you mean business. If you will come right up to the front, we will pray with you and God will meet you. The people would flock to the front. He would exhort them: Who will lift up his hands in faith and ask God for something? Now thank God for it. Now again, ask God for something. Now thank God. The exercise of faith brought the answer to hundreds, and many were baptized in the Spirit as they lifted up their hands and voices to God.

66 *Real faith has perfect peace and joy and a shout at any time. It always sees the victory.*

I believe that there is only one way to all the treasures of God, and that is the way of faith. By faith and faith alone do we enter into a knowledge of the attributes and become partakers of the beatitudes and participate in the glories of our ascended Lord. All His promises are Yea and Amen to them that believe.

Real faith built the ark, but real faith did not shut the door. God did that. He does what you cannot do.

The power of God is beyond all our conception. The trouble is that we do not have the power of God in a full manifestation because of our finite thoughts, but as we go on and let God have His way, there is no limit to what our limitless God will do in response to a limitless faith. But you will never get anywhere except you are in constant pursuit of all the power of God.

The greatest sin in all the world is "unbelief." It will shut everything out from you; it will hinder your progress and blight the prospects of your life. It will shut Heaven and open hell; but if you believe God your faith will shut hell and open Heaven.

Purity is vital to faith. When you throw your whole heart and life into the plan of God, when you long to be holy, when you long to be pure, then and only then will the law of the Spirit of life make you free from the law of sin and death.

There is nothing that our God cannot do. He will do everything if you will dare to believe.

There is no such thing as the Lord not meeting your need. All things are possible to him that believeth.

Dare to believe and then dare to speak and you shall have whatsoever you say if you doubt not.

There are boundless possibilities for us if we dare to act in God and dare to believe!

There are many who call themselves believers who are extremely unbelieving.

Brothers and sisters, as you ask, BELIEVE.

I am not moved by what I see. I am moved only by what I believe. I know this, no man looks at appearances if he believes. No man considers how he feels if he believes. The man who believes God has it.

I saw that God wants us so badly that He has made the condition as simple as He possibly could—Only Believe.

One man in a meeting, filled with unbelief, can make a place for the devil to have a seat.

The blood of Jesus Christ and His mighty Name are an antidote to all the subtle seeds of unbelief that satan would sow in your minds.

When the gift of Faith is in operation you know ahead of time what the Holy Spirit is going to do.

When we believe God, all things are easy.

Have faith in God. Believe the Scripture is for you. If you want a high tide rising in the power of God, say, "Give me, Lord, that which I shall be short in nothing." Have a real faith.

Prayer is without accomplishment unless it is accompanied by faith.

What is faith? It is the very nature of God at work in you. Faith is the Word of God...the personality flowing through you, the character of Jesus is manifested in you.

Believers were designed to operate in what is called: the law of faith.

❝_I believe that all lack of faith is due to not feeding, drinking, thinking, speaking, and singing God's Word!_

To the man of faith everything that is contrary to the will and the Word of God is nothing but an opportunity to prove that God is true.

Faith never fears, faith thrives in the greatest conflict, faith moves even things that cannot be moved.

The man who believes God has it.

I'll only pray for you once, to pray twice is unbelief.

There is something about believing God that will cause Him to pass over a million people to get to you.

Hebrews 11:1 (KJV)
Now faith is the substance of things hoped for, the evidence of things not seen.

CHAPTER 48

Healing

❝*I am never happier in the Lord than when I am in a bedroom with a sick person.*

We can never have the gifts of healing and the working of miracles in operation only as we stand in the Divine power that God gives us, and we stand believing God and having done all we still stand believing.

There is a fruit of the Spirit that must accompany the gift of healing, and that is longsuffering.

Men can grow lopsided by emphasizing the truth of Divine healing. Men can get wrong by all the time preaching on water baptism. But we never go wrong in exalting the Lord Jesus Christ, giving Him the Preeminent Place and magnifying Him as both Lord and Christ, yes, as very God of very God.

James 5:14-16 (KJV)

14 Is any sick among you? let him call for the elders of the church; and let them pray over him, anointing him with oil in the name of the Lord: 15 And the prayer of faith shall save the sick, and the Lord shall raise him up; and if he have committed sins, they shall be forgiven him. 16 Confess your faults one to another, and pray one for another, that ye may be healed. The effectual fervent prayer of a righteous man availeth much.

CHAPTER 49

Holy Spirit

❝I would rather have the Spirit of God on me for five minutes than to receive a million dollars.

I refuse to use a gift unless the Holy Ghost manifests His power to bring the gift through.

Anyone can be ordinary, but a person filled with the Holy Spirit must be extraordinary. The people looked to him for something new, something out of the usual run of things, and they were not disappointed.

If the Spirit does not move me, I move the Holy Spirit.

God wants His people to be ablaze with Holy Ghost activity.

I'd rather have the anointing of God for 10 minutes than to own the whole world with a fence round it.

God can so fill a man with His Spirit that he can laugh and believe in the face of a thousand difficulties.

The plan of God for your life is that you should be held captive by His power, doing that which you in the natural world would never do, but that which you are forced to do by the power of the Holy Ghost moving through you.

The Spirit reveals, unfolds, takes of the things of Christ and shows them to us, and prepares us to be more than a match for satanic forces.

I never get out of bed in the morning without having communion with God in the Spirit.

There is a place where God, through the power of the Holy Ghost, reigns supreme in our lives.

It is impossible to overestimate the importance of being filled with the Spirit.

A man filled with the Holy Spirit is no longer an ordinary man.

I am here to help you to begin doing mighty acts in the power of God through the gifts of the Spirit. The man who is filled with the Holy Spirit is always acting. Jesus had to begin to do, and so must we.

You don't tarry for the Holy Ghost. He has already been given; He is here. You don't tarry; you receive.

Turning for a moment to Jesus' attitude in the Holy Spirit, I would like you to see a plan there. In Acts 1, we find that Jesus began both to do and teach (v. 1); the believer should always be so full of the Holy Spirit that he begins to do, and then he can teach. He must be ready for the man in the street. He must be instantly ready, flowing like a river. He must have three things: ministration, operation, and manifestation, and these three things must always be forthcoming. We ought to be so full of the manifestation of the power of God that, in the name of Jesus, we can absolutely destroy the power of satan.

When our temples are purified and our minds are put in order so that carnalities and fleshly desires and everything contrary to the Spirit have gone, then the Holy Spirit can take full charge.

The Holy Spirit is not a manifestation of carnality.

If you deal in the flesh after you are baptized in the Holy Spirit, you cease to go on.

When the Holy Spirit comes into your body, He comes to unveil the King, to assure you of His presence.

The Holy Spirit is coming to take out of the world a Church that is a perfect bride. He must find in us perfect yieldedness, with every desire subjected to Him.

❝When the Holy Spirit comes, He will reveal things to you. Has He revealed them yet? He is going to do it. Just expect Him to do so. The best thing for you is to expect Him to do it now.

We must be careful not to choose, but to let God's Holy Spirit manage our lives; not to smooth down and explain away, but to stir up the gift and allow God's Spirit to disturb us and disturb us and disturb us until we yield and yield and yield and the possibility in God's mind for us becomes an established fact in our lives, with the rivers in evidence meeting the need of a dying world.

Life comes after you have been filled with the Holy Spirit. Get down and pray for power.

I believe that God wants to put His hand upon us so that we may reach ideal definitions of humility, of human helplessness, of human insufficiency, until we will rest no more upon human plans, but have God's thoughts, God's voice, and the Holy Spirit to speak to us.

God longs intensively for unhindered communication and total response between Him, and the believer indwelt by the Holy Spirit.

Many Christians think that they are obedient because they do not overtly sin by disobeying the rules – the do's and don'ts. But this is not all there is to it. We must realize that God, the Holy Spirit, is ever waiting to guide us, to draw us away from the distractions and sinfulness of our surroundings just to bring us into fellowship with Him.

If you want to increase in the life of God, then you must settle it in your heart that you will not at any time resist the Holy Spirit. The Holy Ghost and fire - the fire burning up everything that would impoverish and destroy you.

As we are filled with the Holy Spirit our one desire is to magnify Him. We need to be filled with the Spirit to get the full revelation of the Lord Jesus Christ.

Divine life is full of Divine appointment and equipping, and you cannot be filled with the power of God without a manifestation. It is my prayer that we would understand that to be filled with the Holy Spirit is to be filled with manifestation, the glory of the Lord being in the midst of us, manifesting His Divine power.

Possess patience to such an extent that you can suffer anything for the Church, for your friends, for your neighbors, or for anyone. Remember this: we build character in others as our character is built. As we are pure in our thoughts, are tender and gracious to other people, and possess our souls in patience, then people have a great desire for our fellowship in the Holy Spirit.

Every day the child of God must be moved more and more by the Holy Ghost. The child of God must come into line with the power of Heaven so that he knows that God has His hand upon him.

God wants his people ablaze with Holy Ghost activity.

I am on the plan of daring, acting in the Holy Ghost.

Some like to read the Bible in the Hebrew. Some in the Greek. I like to read it in the Holy Ghost.

Enter into the promises of God. It is your inheritance. You will do more in one year if you are really filled with the Holy Ghost than you could do in fifty years apart from Him.

Repeat in your heart often baptized with the Holy Ghost and fire, fire, fire! All the unction, and weeping, and travailing comes through the baptism of fire, and I say to you and say to myself, purged and cleansed and filled with renewed spiritual power.

66 *The Holy Spirit takes it for granted that you are finished with all the things of the old, like when you become a new creation in Christ.*

When you receive the Holy Ghost you receive God's Gift, in whom are all the gifts of the Spirit.

God wants to purify our minds until we can bear all things, believe all things, hope all things, and endure all things. God dwells in you, but you cannot have this Divine power until you live and walk in the Holy Ghost, until the power of the new life is greater than the old life.

Wherever the Holy Ghost has right of way, the gifts of the Spirit will be in manifestation; and where these gifts are never in manifestation, I question whether He is present.

The secret for the future is living and moving in the power of the Holy Ghost.

When things are not going right, there are satanic forces in operation. What is my solution? To rebuke the condition of sin, death, disease, or whatever it is. I can pray in the Holy Ghost, and that prayer is effectual to bring down every stronghold of the enemy.

The plan of God for your life is that you should be held captive by His power, doing that which you in the natural world would never do, but that which you are forced to do by the power of the Holy Ghost moving through you.

There is a place where God, through the power of the Holy Ghost, reigns supreme in our lives.

Life comes after you have been filled with the Holy Ghost, get down and pray for power.

It is an insult to ask God for power after you have received the baptism of the Holy Ghost. You have power! You have to ACT!

These times of waiting on God for the fullness of the Spirit are times when He searches the heart and tests the mind.

If we see the truth as clearly as God intends for us to see it, we will all be made so much richer, looking forward to the Blessed One who is coming again. Here we are, face-to-face with the facts. God has shown us different aspects of the Spirit. He has shown us the pavilion.

Praise is God's sunlight in the heart. It destroys sin germs. It ripens the fruits of the Spirit. It is the oil of gladness that lubricates life's activities.

Be filled to overflowing with the Spirit. We are no good if we have only a full cup; we need to have an overflowing cup!

Jesus was totally yielded and obedient to the Father, and therefore, God did not give the Spirit by measure to Him. God's Spirit was upon Him without limit, and He moved in unlimited power. Jesus showed us by His example, the way to walk in power.

I am all Pentecost.

We must move away from everything that pertains to the letter. All that we do must be done under the anointing of the Spirit.

There is something about believing in God that makes God willing to pass over a million people just to anoint you.

When I catch the first breath of the Spirit, I leave everything and everybody to be in His presence, to hear what He has to say to me.

❝It is impossible to overestimate the importance of being filled with the Spirit.

The Spirit reveals, unfolds, takes of the things of Christ and shows them to us, and prepares us to be more than a match for satanic forces.

Pentecost came with the sound of a mighty rushing wind, a violent blast from Heaven! Heaven has not exhausted its blasts, but our danger is we are getting frightened of them.

There are two sides to this Baptism: The first is, you possess the Spirit; the second is that the Spirit possesses you.

Never get out of bed in the morning without having communion with God in the Spirit.

Be filled with the Spirit, be crammed with the Spirit, so filled that there will be no room left for anything else. What is the advantage of such a life? We can only feel what reaches the central realm of consciousness.

The Lord will allow you to be very drunk in His presence but sober among people.

If you want to know the mind of God, you must have the Holy Ghost to bring God's latest thought to you and to tell you what to do.

When the power of the Holy Ghost is present, things will happen.

Ephesians 5:18 (KJV)
And be not drunk with wine, wherein is excess; but be filled with the Spirit;

CHAPTER 50

⋯⋯

Laughter

❝God can so fill a man with His Spirit that he can laugh and believe in the face of a thousand difficulties.

I am not here to entertain you, but to get you to the place where you will laugh at the impossible.

Faith laughs at impossibilities, and cries, "It shall be done!"

Laughter in the Holy Ghost brings you out of everything!

God wants to impart to us a faith that can laugh at impossibilities and rest in peace.

It may seem to some people very strange, but I have seen people come into a meeting down and out, exhausted. The power of God has come on them with laughter. Laughter in the Holy Ghost brings you out of everything! It is a thing you cannot create. The Holy Ghost laughs through you. You laugh from the inside. The whole body is so full of the Spirit of life from above that you are altogether new. For

God to come into a needy soul and create laughter within is very wonderful.

Faith, when it is moved by the power of God, can laugh when there is trouble.

If you are sure of your ground, if you are counting on the presence of the living Christ within, you can laugh when you see things getting worse.

Psalm 126:1-2 (KJV)
1 When the Lord turned again the captivity of Zion,
We were like them that dream. 2 Then was our mouth
Filled with laughter, and our tongue with singing:
then said they among the heathen,
The Lord hath done great things for them.

CHAPTER 51

Ministry

❝If I leave you as I found you, I am not God's channel.

We must see the face of the Lord. There are things that God says to me that I know must take place. It doesn't matter what people say. I have been face to face with some of the most trying moments of men's lives when it meant so much to me if I kept the vision, and if I held fast to that which God had said. A man must be in an immovable condition. The voice of God must mean to him more than what he sees, feels, or what people say.

If you seek nothing but the will of God, He will always put you in the right place at the right time.

God does not call those who are equipped, He equips those whom He has called.

You are in the right position when you allow the glory of the new life to cause you to act. Live in the Acts of the Apostles, and every day you will see some miracle worked by the power of the living God.

God has never sent me anywhere too late.

Oh, if God had His way, we would be like torches, purifying the very atmosphere wherever we go, moving back the forces of wickedness.

Oh, the name of Jesus! There is power in that Name to meet every condition of human need.

Now, beloved, I am out for men. It is my business to be out for men. It is my business to make everybody hungry and dissatisfied. It is my business to make people either glad or mad. I have a message from Heaven that will not leave people as I find them.

If you leave people as you found them, God is not speaking by you. If you are not making people mad or glad, there is something amiss with your ministry. If there is not a war on, it's a bad job for you.

God wants manifestation, and He wants His glory to be seen. You are going to miss a great deal if you don't begin to act.

A preacher must not tell his audiences what he thinks but what he knows and let them do the thinking.

Jesus saw every touch by God as a miracle.

God has chosen us to help one another.

The man who wants to work the works of God must never look at conditions but at Jesus.

The power of God is just the same today as it was in the past.

God is here this morning in power, in blessing, and saying to you, what is your request? Oh, He is so precious! He never fails.

Power from on high. It is God inserting into you, Divine activity with mightiness.

2 Timothy 4:5 (KJV)
But watch thou in all things, endure afflictions, do the work of an evangelist, make full proof of thy ministry.

CHAPTER 52

✦

Prayer

66 **I don't often spend more than half an hour in prayer at one time, but I never go more than half an hour without praying.**

If you ask God seven times for the same thing, six times are in unbelief.

God is more eager to answer, than we are to ask.

I can get more out of God by believing Him for one minute than by shouting at Him all night.

You will have to voice many things in order to bring them into being.

God will come to the one who cries first.

Voice your position in God and you will be surrounded by all the resources of God in the time of trial.

I will tell you, for I never saw a man get anything from God who prayed on the earth. If you get anything from God, you will have to pray into Heaven; for it is all there. If you are living in the earth realm and expect things from Heaven, they will never come.

God has never changed the order of things that first, there comes the natural, and then the spiritual. For instance, when it is on your heart to pray, you begin in the natural and your second word will probably be under the power of the Spirit. You begin and God will end.

We must have reality, the real working of our God. We must know God. We must be able to go in and hold converse with God. We must also know the mind of God toward us, so that all our petitions are always on the line of His will.

We miss the grandeur because we lack audacity. If you will voice God at any time, you will find Him greater than any power that is round about you.

Luke 18:1 (KJV)
And he spake a parable unto them to this end, that men ought always to pray, and not to faint;

CHAPTER 53

Purity

❝ **To hunger and thirst after righteousness is when nothing in the world can fascinate us so much as being near God.**

You must every day make higher ground. You must deny yourself to make progress with God. You must refuse everything that is not pure and holy. God wants you pure in heart. He wants you to have an intense desire after holiness.

The moment a man falls into sin, Divine life ceases to flow, and his life becomes one of helplessness.

One half of the trouble in the assemblies is the people's murmuring over the conditions they are in. The Bible teaches us not to murmur. If you reach that standard, you will never murmur anymore. You will be above murmuring. You will be in the place where God is absolutely the exchanger of thought, the exchanger of actions, and the exchanger of your inward purity. He will be purifying you all the time and lifting you higher, and you will know you are not of this world.

Those who carry the vessels of the Lord must be clean, must be holy.

We are saved, called with a holy calling-called to be saints, holy, pure, God-like, sons with power.

God wants us to let the mind that was in Christ Jesus, that pure, holy, humble mind of Christ, be in us.

The Lord would so cleanse the motive and desires of our hearts that we will seek but one thing only, and that is, His glory.

Oh, for an inward savor that shall make us say "A thousand deaths rather than sinning once." O Jesus, we worship Thee! Thou art worthy!

Matthew 5:8 (KJV)
Blessed are the pure in heart: for they shall see God.

CHAPTER 54

⁌⁍

Tongues

❝Smith Wigglesworth was asked why he didn't take vacations or holidays. He replied, "I do. I take a holiday every day. I pray in other tongues, and I am refreshed and rested and ready to continue working in the Fathers vineyard."

Smith Wigglesworth washing himself in speaking in tongues - refers to a powerful imagery used to describe his fervent and intense prayer life where he would reportedly immerse himself in speaking in tongues, often to the point of being completely absorbed in the spiritual experience, almost as if "washing" himself in the flow of the Holy Spirit through this practice.

Do not rest satisfied with any lesser experience than the baptism that the disciples received on the Day of Pentecost.

After the Holy Spirit comes in, it is impossible to keep your tongue still.

Smith Wigglesworth would pray in tongues for two hours a day, and he called it washing himself in speaking in tongues.

As the dead body of Christ was given life and brought out by the Holy Spirit, may we be given eyes to see, ears to hear, and a tongue to speak as the oracles of God.

Every person, whoever he is, who receives the Holy Spirit will have prophetic utterances in the Spirit unto God or in a human man language supernaturally coming forth, so that all the people will know that it is the Spirit.

And I went up and down Fleet Street and the Strand, lost in the Spirit, in tongues all the time. It was lovely.

After the Holy Spirit comes in, a man is in a new order in God. You will find it so real that you will want to sing, talk, laugh, and shout.

We are in a strange place when the Holy Spirit comes in. If the incoming of the Spirit is lovely, what must be the outflow? The incoming is only to be an outflow.

What we need is more of the Holy Spirit. Oh, beloved, it is not merely a measure of the Spirit; it is a pressed-down measure. It is not merely a pressed down measure; it is 'shaken together and running over' (Luke 6: 38).

Through this wonderful Baptism in the Spirit, which the Lord gives us, He enables us to talk to Himself in a language that the Spirit has given, a language which no man understands but which He understands, a language of love.

Oh, how wonderful it is to speak to Him in the Spirit, to let the Spirit lift and lift and lift us until he takes us into the very presence of God!

When we are praying in the Holy Ghost, faith is in evidence, and as a result, the power of God can be manifested in our midst.

It is a wonderful thing to pray in the Spirit and to sing in the Spirit, praying in tongues and singing in tongues as the Spirit of God gives you utterance.

I believe in the Baptism of the Holy Ghost with the speaking in tongues, and I believe that every man who is baptized in the Holy Ghost will speak in other tongues as the Spirit gives him utterance.

❝God has ordained this speaking in an unknown tongue unto Himself as a wonderful, supernatural means of communication in the Spirit.

I thank God He baptizes with the Holy Ghost. I know He did it for me because they heard me speak in tongues, and then I heard myself.

There are great possibilities as we yield to the Spirit and speak unto God in quiet hours in our bedrooms. God wants you to be filled with the Holy Ghost so that everything about you shall be charged with the dynamic of heaven.

And He gives me language that I cannot speak fast enough; it comes too fast, and it is there because God has given it.

We must be edified before we can edify the church. I cannot estimate what I, personally, owe to the Holy Ghost method of spiritual edification.

When the Comforter is come, He shall teach you ALL things, and He has given me this supernatural means of speaking in an unknown tongue to edify myself so that, after being edified, I can edify the church.

As you rise up in the morning, believe this wonderful truth, and as you yield to the Spirit's presence and power, you will find yourself speaking unto God in the Spirit, and you will find that you are personally being edified by doing this.

It is most lovely to be in the Spirit when you are dressing, and you come out to the world, and the world has no effect on you. You begin the day like that, and you will be conscious of the guidance of the Spirit right through the day.

1 Corinthians 14:2
For he that speaketh in an unknown tongue speaketh not unto men, but unto God: for no man understandeth him; howbeit in the spirit he speaketh mysteries.

CHAPTER 55

Warfare

❝ *Shout, 'Get thee behind me, satan,' and you will have the best time on earth. Whisper it, and you won't.*

We are nothing in ourselves, but in Christ we are more than conquerors through the blood of Jesus—more than a match for satanic powers in every way.

If you have a great God, you will have a little devil, and if you have a big devil, you will have a little God.

The devil will endeavor to fascinate through the eyes and through the mind.

When you take authority over the devil in any situation, what counts is what the devil sees. If he only sees the uncommitted you, like the seven sons of Sceva, you're in trouble.

Temptations will come to all. If you are not worth tempting, you are not worth much.

There are evil powers, but Jesus is greater than all evil powers. There are tremendous diseases, but Jesus is healer. There is no case too hard for Him. The Lion of Judah shall break every chain. He came to relieve the oppressed and to set the captive free. He came to bring redemption, to make us as perfect as man was before the fall.

1 Peter 5:8 (KJV)
Be sober, be vigilant; because your adversary the devil, as a roaring lion, walketh about, seeking whom he may devour:

CHAPTER 56

Word of God

❝ The Word of God has not to be prayed about, the Word of God has to be received.

By the grace of God, I want to impart the Word and bring you to a place where you will dare to act on it.

Let everything about you be a lie but let this Word of God be true.

If a thing is in the Bible, then it is so; it is not even to be prayed about; it is to be received and acted upon.

There are four principles we need to maintain: First, read the Word of God. Second, consume the Word of God until it consumes you. Third believe the Word of God. Fourth, act on the Word.

There is power in God's Word to make that which does not exist appear.

I want to impart the word to you to get you to a place where you will laugh at the impossible.

The Word of God will bring you into a wonderful place of rest in faith.

I find nothing in the Bible but holiness, and nothing in the world but worldliness. Therefore, if I live in the world, I will become worldly; on the other hand, if I live in the Bible, I will become holy.

Nothing in the world glorifies God so much as simple rest of faith in what God's Word says.

The Word of God is eternal and cannot be broken. You cannot improve on the Word of God, for it is life and it produces only life.

It is one thing to know the Word, and another thing to be captive to the Word. You are either captive to the Word, or captive to the world.

You have to bring your mind to the Word of God and not try to bring the Word of God to your mind.

The Bible is the Word of God: supernatural in origin, eternal in duration, inexpressible in valor, infinite in scope, regenerative in power, infallible in authority, universal in interest, personal in application, inspired in totality. Read it through, write it down, pray it in, work it out, and then pass it on. Truly it is the Word of God. It brings into man the personality of God; it changes the man until he becomes the epistle of God. It transforms his mind, changes his character, takes him on from grace to grace, and gives him an inheritance in the Spirit. God comes in, dwells in, walks in, talks through, and sups with him.

This blessed Book brings such life and health and peace, and such abundance that we should never be poor anymore.

You must be yielded to the Word of God. The Word will work out love in our hearts, and when practical love is in our hearts, there is no room to boast about ourselves. We see ourselves as nothing when we get lost in this Divine love.

It is as we feed on the Word and meditate on the message it contains that the Spirit of God can vitalize that which we have received, and bring forth through us the word of knowledge that will be as full of power and life as when He, the Spirit of God, moved upon holy men of old and gave them these inspired Scriptures.

God's Word never fails. He will always heal you if you dare to believe Him. Men are searching everywhere today for things with which they can heal themselves, and they ignore the fact that the Balm of Gilead is within easy reach.

I can't understand God by feelings. I can't understand the Lord Jesus Christ by feelings. I can only understand God the Father and Jesus Christ by what the Word says about them. God is everything the Word says He is. We need to get acquainted with Him through the Word.

❝ When the saint ceases to seek after holiness, purity, righteousness, truth; when he ceases to pray, stops reading the Word and gives way to carnal appetites, then it is that satan comes.

If I read the newspaper, I come out dirtier than I went in. If I read my Bible, I come out cleaner than I went in, and I like being clean!

None of you can be strong in God unless you are diligently and constantly hearkening to what God has to say to you through His Word.

Libraries make swelled heads, but the Word of God makes enlarged hearts.

Faith cometh by hearing, and hearing by the Word of God - not by reading commentaries.

Fill your head and your heart with the Scriptures. As you do this, you are sowing in your heart seeds which the Spirit can germinate.

Believers are strong only as the Word of God abides in them.

Never compare this book with other books. Comparisons are dangerous. Never think or say that this book contains the Word of God. IT IS the Word of God. It is supernatural in origin, eternal in duration, inexpressible in value, infinite in scope, regenerative in power, infallible in authority, universal in interest, personal in application, and inspired in totality. Read it through, write it down, pray it in and pass it on. It is the Word of God.

If you will receive the Word of God, you will always be in a big place.

It is absolutely infidelity and unbelief to pray about anything in the Word of God.

Ephesians 6:17 (KJV)
And take the helmet of salvation, and the sword of the Spirit, which is the word of God:

CHAPTER 57

Miscellaneous

❝I want to help you decide that, by the power of God, you will not be ordinary.

Everyone in this place who is saved has a million times more than they know.

It is better to live ready than to get ready!

Great faith is the product of great fights. Great testimonies are the outcome of great tests. Great triumphs can only come out of great trials.

A man is in a great place when he has no one to turn to but God.

The power of God will take you out of your own plans and put you into the plan of God.

If you seek nothing but the will of God, He will always put you in the right place at the right time.

To hunger and thirst after righteousness is when nothing in the world can fascinate us so much as being near God.

Live in the Acts of the Apostles, and every day you will see some miracle worked by the power of the living God.

There are boundless possibilities for us if we dare to act in God and dare to believe!

If I leave you as I found you, I am not God's channel.

In me is working a power stronger than every other power. The life that is in me is a thousand times bigger than I am outside.

The devil knows if he can capture your thought life he has won a mighty victory over you.

When the saint ceases to seek after holiness, purity, righteousness, truth; when he ceases to pray, stops reading the Word and gives way to carnal appetites, then it is that satan comes.

Whatever God has done for other men, He can do for me.

To live two days in succession on the same spiritual plane is a tragedy.

The moment a man falls into sin, Divine life ceases to flow, and his life becomes one of helplessness.

There is power to overcome everything in the world through the Name of Jesus.

It pays to trust God with all and to make no reservation.

I am satisfied with the dissatisfaction that never rests until it is satisfied and satisfied again.

❝ *Put this right in your mind and never forget it: you will never be any importance to God till you venture into the impossible. God wants people on the daring line. I do not mean foolish daring.*

The most difficult things that come to us are to our advantage from God's side. When we come to the place of impossibilities, it is the grandest place for us to see the possibilities of God.

The lack today is the lack of understanding of that blessed fullness of Christ.

My Heavenly bank, my Heavenly bank, the house of God's treasure and store. I have plenty in here; I'm a real millionaire.

So, I have an extravagant God with extravagant language to make me an extravagant person-in wisdom.

All the saints of God who get the real vision of this wonderful transformation are seeing every day that the world is getting worse and worse. It is ripening for Judgment.

It is when you get out of the will of God that you have a hard time.

You must come to see how wonderful you are in God, and how helpless you are in yourself.

Perfect love will never want the preeminence in everything, it will never want to take the place of another, it will always be willing to take the back seat.

Whatever God has done for other men, He can do for me.

Every stumbling block must become a steppingstone, and every opposition must become an opportunity.

Do more believing and less begging.

Remember this: You never lose so much as when you lose your peace. If the people see that you have lost your groundwork of peace, they know you have got outside of the position of victory. You have to possess your soul in peace.

O God, give us such a holy, intense, Divine acquaintance that we would rather die than grieve Thee!

I like anything that God does.

I like to watch God working.

No man can doubt if he will learn to shout.

Romans 16:20 (KJV)
And the God of peace shall bruise Satan under your feet shortly. The grace of our Lord Jesus Christ be with you. Amen.

About the Author

Vince Baker was born in Southern California and later lived on 17 acres just north of Sacramento. As a child, Vince was raised as a Southern Baptist. Vince was always drawn to the Lord and even said he wanted to be a preacher at an early age.

Vince's life was uneventful until, one day, he encountered God while driving in his car at the age of 17. God manifested Himself to Vince so powerfully that his life would never be the same. After this experience, Vince became a Christian and dedicated his life to the Lord. In that same month, Vince received a book from his Christian Grandma called **"The Secret of His Power."** This book was about a famous miracle-working Evangelist named Smith Wigglesworth. God used this book to prepare Vince for ministry. God also used Smith's testimony, which was found in another book called "Apostle of Faith," to talk to him about things He wanted to do through him in his later years.

Vince decided to go to a Christian high school in his senior year. At this school, Vince was introduced to a seasoned Evangelist who took local churches to feed the poor and evangelize. Vince found out he lived near the Evangelist and started traveling with him. During this time, Vince became his right-hand man and saw many profound miracles on the streets through this ministry. This ministry was called to train the Church on evangelizing with power. Vince traveled up and down the West Coast, ministering to the homeless and helpless while equipping the Church. Vince has a big heart for the poor, homeless, and hurting people.

Within a short time, Vince heard from God to attend Bible College. Through confirmation from God and a miracle of his tuition being paid for, Vince started to study the Bible more deeply at this Bible College. Vince's foundational training from the Word of God during this time was priceless. Vince ended up graduating as the Valedictorian from this Bible College.

After Bible College, Vince started ministering to kids at a Christian school, taught Sunday School, and functioned in the local Church. Vince later moved into full-time ministry and was an assistant Pastor at a local Church for five years during the mid-'90s.

As an assistant Pastor, Vince visited a Church where the Prophet Kim Clement was ministering. Prophet Kim Clement pulled Vince out of the crowd and prophesied over him. In that prophecy, God told Vince through Kim Clement that He would use him mightily and needed to prepare himself.

Vince later worked in the marketplace, where he was the CEO and part-owner of Agora Advantage. God called Vince to the marketplace, but Vince knew that he would be called back into full-time ministry later in life. Agora Advantage has been a fantastic position where Vince has grown in many ways. As a sign from God, Vince was voted in as the CEO of Agora Advantage on the Day of Pentecost.

As Vince neared the prophesied time that God would bring him back into full-time ministry, he began seeking the Lord more deeply. During this time, Vince had another unforgettable encounter with God regarding the Ark of the Covenant. God gave Vince a vision of four men carrying the Ark of the Covenant into a Church. The Holy Spirit spoke to Vince and said, "Wherever you read Ark of the Covenant in the Old Testament, think Holy Spirit. Wherever you read Holy Spirit in the New Testament, think Ark of the Covenant. Put the two together, and you will know Me." Vince studied these two subjects everywhere he could find them in the Bible and received tremendous insight into understanding the Holy Spirit.

God also revealed to Vince a prophetic way to study the Bible from this experience. Vince went on to spend years in the Word of God, studying different subjects of the Bible as the Holy Spirit led him. At the leading of the Holy Spirit, Vince researched every place a word or phrase was found from the Old and New Testaments. Vince has currently done over four hundred of these studies, some of which took months to complete. The revelations that came out of these studies were life-changing. Vince wrote down all these teachings and revelations, which make up many of the truths he writes about in his books and preaches in his messages today. Vince found that when you study a subject everywhere it is located in the Bible, and you can receive the full counsel of God on that subject. Vince also received many dreams and visitations from God during this time.

Vince has a unique calling where he can preach, teach, prophecy, move in the gifts of the Spirit, bring healing, and perform miracles by the power of the Holy Spirit. Vince is called to help the body of Christ come into their destiny and High Calling.

Currently, Vince resides in Northern California with his wife, Eunice, and their two dogs, who are enjoying the blessings of God.

Invite Vince to Speak

Visit

www.VinceBakerMinistries.com

ADDITIONAL BOOK BY
VINCE BAKER

221

ADDITIONAL BOOK BY
VINCE BAKER

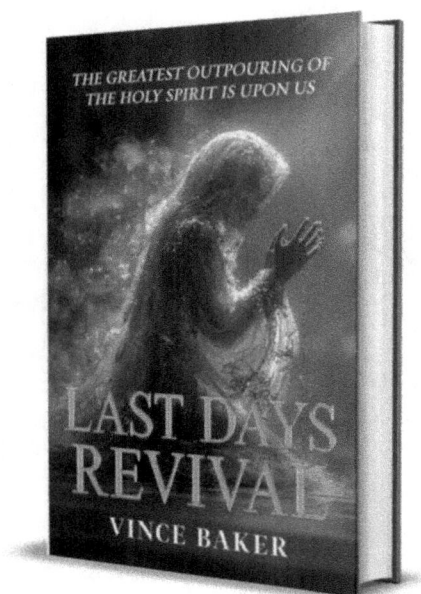

ADDITIONAL BOOK BY
VINCE BAKER

ADDITIONAL BOOK BY
VINCE BAKER

ADDITIONAL BOOK BY
VINCE BAKER

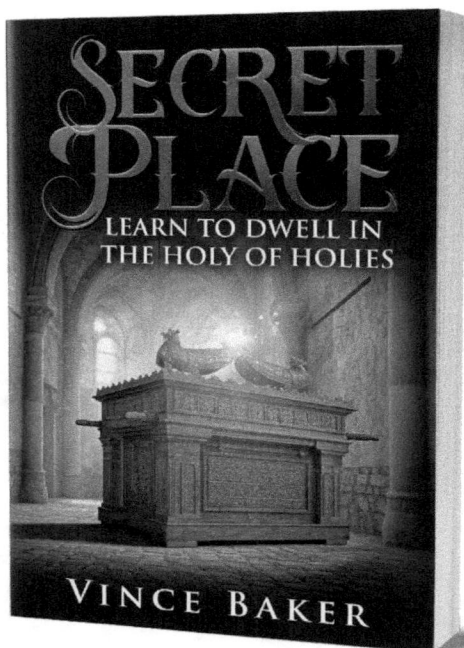

ADDITIONAL BOOK BY
VINCE BAKER

ADDITIONAL BOOK BY VINCE BAKER

ADDITIONAL BOOK BY
VINCE BAKER

ADDITIONAL BOOK BY VINCE BAKER

ADDITIONAL BOOK BY
VINCE BAKER

231

ADDITIONAL BOOK BY
VINCE BAKER

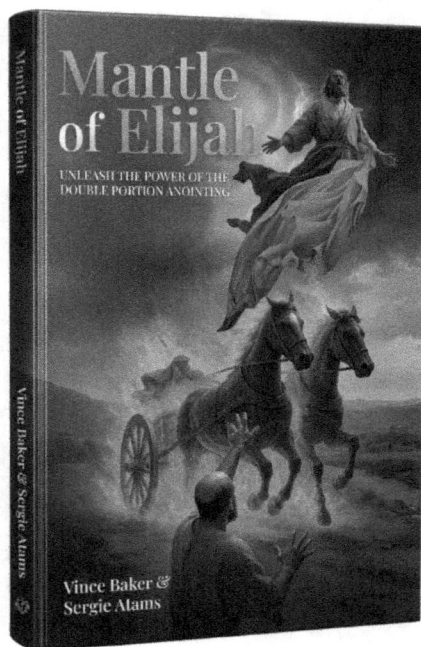

ADDITIONAL BOOK BY
VINCE BAKER

www.amazon.com/author/vincebaker

www.VinceBakerMinistries.com

ADDITIONAL BOOK BY
VINCE BAKER

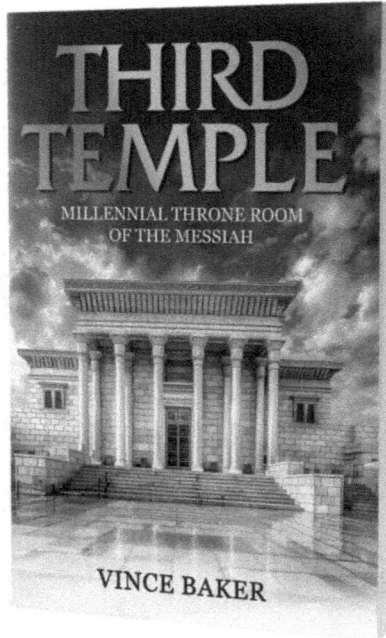

ADDITIONAL BOOK BY
VINCE BAKER

ADDITIONAL BOOK BY VINCE BAKER